Help Your Marriage Survive the Death of a Child

Paul C. Rosenblatt

 Temple University Press
Philadelphia

Temple University Press, Philadelphia 19122
Copyright © 2000 by Temple University
All rights reserved
Published 2000
Printed in the United States of America

♾ The paper used in this publication meets the requirements of the
American National Standard for Information Sciences–Permanence
of Paper for Printed Library Materials, ANSI Z39.48-1984.

Library of Congress Cataloging-in-Publication Data

Rosenblatt, Paul C.
   Help your marriage survive the death of a child / Paul C. Rosenblatt.
     p. cm.
   Includes bibliographical references and index.
   ISBN 1-56639-804-5 (hardcover: alk. paper) – ISBN 1-56639-805-3
(pbk.: alk. paper)
    1. Married couples–United States–Psychology. 2. Married
couples–United States–Family relationships. 3. Children–United
States–Mortality. 4. Bereavement–United States. 5. Loss
(Psychology)–United States. 6. Communication in marriage–
United States. I. Title.

HQ536.R657   2000
306.872–dc21   00-029941

To all the children who have died,
we remember you.

To all the parents,
the ones quoted in this book,
the others who have talked with me,
and the millions of others
who have experienced
the death of a child.

Contents

Acknowledgments

MY WORK on this book benefited from financial support from the Agricultural Experiment Station of the University of Minnesota and a year's sabbatical leave from the university. My two department heads, Hal Grotevant and Jan Hogan, helped in many ways, perhaps most of all by providing an environment that values books like this.

I had excellent interviewing help from Terri Karis and Anna Hagemeister. Over the years of dreaming about this book, carrying out the interviews, and writing, many people provided sustaining interest, conversation, ideas, and stories. In particular, I thank Sara Wright, Janice Nadeau, Shais and Rochel Rosenblatt, Anna Hagemeister, Terri Karis, Jeanne K. Hanson, John Jung, Dennis Klass, Kathy Gilbert, Paul Lasley, Ramona Oswald, Jennifer Daniel, Ronit Leichtentritt, and Emily Wright-Rosenblatt. Most of all, I was helped by the bereaved parents whose stories are the heart of this book and whose belief in the importance of a book like this kept me moving forward.

Help Your Marriage
Survive the Death of a Child

1

"It's the Hardest Thing We Ever Had to Go Through"

MY FIRST GRANDSON, Eli, died when he was two. He was sick beyond repair within an hour of being born. All the days he struggled to stay alive, I ached for him. I ached for my son and daughter-in-law. They loved Eli enormously and were locked in a grinding around-the-clock vigil to keep him breathing and as healthy as he could be. After Eli died I hurt, much more for my son and daughter-in-law than for Eli or myself.

As things turned out, my son and daughter-in-law had wonderful resources in themselves, in their relationship, and in their community to help them cope, but Eli's death got me wondering about couples who have a more difficult time of it. I knew from the research literature and my own previous work that many bereaved parents struggle for a lifetime with personal and marital issues related to a child's dying. Where can they go for help with their couple relationship? When I looked in bookstores and libraries for books that could help couples deal with marital problems connected to a child's death, I knew this book was necessary.

I found lots of books on individual parent grief, and some books had a few pages or even a chapter on the couple relationship, but I could find no book that spoke in depth about the many challenging and complex problems couples can have when a child dies. No book examined in much detail what might go on in a couple relationship following a child's death. No book offered much advice on what to do when things seem to be going wrong in a couple's marriage. This book attempts to fill that void.

For many years before I started writing this book, I had been teaching about family relationships at the University of Minnesota and had been researching, writing about, and teaching about grief. I knew the research literature, and it certainly gave me many ideas about what belonged in this book, but I needed to know more. So I set out to interview couples who had had a child die. The twenty-nine couples whose stories of their child's death, their grieving, and their marriage are central to this work all volunteered after learning about my project.

Imagine going with me to do the interview. The setting might be a well cared-for middle-class suburban home, an old farmhouse, a small apartment in an older part of the city, or an expensive home with a long driveway and a kitchen bigger than most living rooms. We sit down with the couple in the kitchen, the living room, or the family room. They offer us coffee or something else to drink. They are obviously tense and eager to start. I turn on the tape recorder and begin asking for background information, questions that help us to know who they are and help them to relax. When we finish with those questions, I ask about the child who died and the story of the death. Most couples start out with an almost objective neutrality, a report of facts, but their story always becomes emotional and personal. It is obviously a story they have thought about many times. And even decades after the death, it brings up strong feelings.

Typically the interview lasts two to four hours. The couple talks a lot about grief, about their relationship with each other, and their relationship with others. There are almost always tears. There is almost always laughter, too. As we get ready to leave, I thank the couple, and often they thank me and say that they had rarely or never had the opportunity to tell the full story.

For me, each interview is a powerful spiritual experience. Each couple tells so much about how they have faced and wrestled with deep and demanding questions about death and life, their struggles to communicate with, understand, and be a partner with each other, the meaning of their child's life and death, and the meaning of life. What they talk about and their accompanying passion could stir up deep feelings in anyone. The emotions their words stir up can penetrate to the core of anyone's heart and soul. I wish you had been there, but I hope this book will give you a strong sense of what you would have learned by sitting in on those interviews.

The children who died ranged in age from three days to thirty-three years. Some of the children had been born so prematurely that they could not survive. There were children who died from genetic disorders, birth defects, accidents, sudden infant death syndrome, suicide, cerebral aneurysm, cancer, and causes nobody could be sure of. Some couples had lost more than one child. Some also talked about children who died of miscarriage or stillbirth, and what they had to say about those losses is included in this book. The time between a couple's most recent child death and the interview ranged from a few months to thirty-five years. (At the end of this book is an appendix with a brief description of the couples and the deaths they talked about, which may help you to keep track of the couples as I quote them throughout the book.)

One of the twenty-nine couples had divorced, one was separated and divorcing, one was separated but not planning to divorce, and two had been separated for months but were together again. Except for the divorced couple and the couple that was divorcing, all couples were interviewed together. The people who were interviewed ranged in age from thirty-three to sixty-eight and in formal education from eighth grade to Ph.D. Maybe what is most important to say about them, however, is that these are people who know what it is like for a child to die. If you have had a child die, they can empathize with you.

Nothing I write here is intended to say, "This is how you should be," or "this is guaranteed to solve your problems." The ideas are suggestions, possibilities, things to think about, ways to look at where you and your spouse have been, are, and may be going. I hope this book will help you to be patient with the long and difficult grief process, to find greater mutual understanding and a shared sense of the enormous range of what can occur in a grieving couple's relationship, to communicate better, and to find ideas that will help you on your shared journey.

A Child's Death Changes Everything

The death of a child not only changes a parent forever, it also permanently alters a couple's marriage. As individuals you must each deal with the awesome, confusing, and painful thoughts and hard and often agonizing and overwhelming feelings that come with a child's death. As a couple you must deal with how each of you has changed. In a sense, you each have become something of a stranger to yourself and each other. And in the process, your marriage cannot be what it was before. It is the marriage of two people who have shared a very heavy loss, of two people who have seen each other grieving, of two people who have gone through the relationship struggles couples experience when a child dies.

You become new people, with no sense of whether you can or should return to being your old selves. You are likely to be beginners at dealing with the kind of grief parents feel and beginners at coming to terms, as a couple, with whatever is going on in you as individuals and as a couple. For quite a while, grief is likely to sap you and your partner of energy to solve problems, to talk about things, to think things through well, and to come to terms with what has happened. For weeks, months, or even years, you may feel that you are in some kind of holding pattern, just trying to do the bare minimum to get along.

Also, your child's death makes you different from most people you know. Although several million American couples have lost a child, you may not know anyone whose experiences can be a resource to you. In fact, your friends, relatives, neighbors, coworkers, and the people in your religious congregation, if you belong to one, may not be able or willing to help beyond the first outpouring of sympathy. Most will never have had a similar experience and most, even if they care for you deeply, will not be very comfortable with you.

Added to all this, grieving can make your couple relationship difficult. Being down so much, being needy and looking at everything in new ways after a child dies, it is easy for you and your spouse to see many negatives in each other and in your marriage that may have been ignored or were not present in the past. So in addition to dealing with the loss of a child, you may have to deal with whether and how to change your marital relationship or even with the possible loss of your marriage.

Hannah: You do a lot of searching. Things come to the surface that you wouldn't think about, unless something happened. Our marital problems have always been there, but they're more on the surface because of what we've been through. I don't know what's gonna happen. It's kind of a shame to throw away thirty years. The problems that we are having have always (*Fred:* [quietly] Yeah) been there. We just never dealt with them before.

Your child's death also may open you as individuals and as a couple to examine and change values, perspectives, and what counts the most for you. You may be moving toward new perspectives on the meaning of life and on what is important.

Elaine: Things that were so important the week before Kyle died were not important at all anymore. Our oldest daughter got pregnant before she was married. At one point in my life that would have been the most devastating thing that could have ever happened. But it was like, what is that in comparison to losing? I'd rather have her that way than not have her at all. Sure, you wished it didn't happen, but how could we not think that this little girl isn't the be all and end all?

* * * * *

Ted: Any experience like that is going to make you appreciate life that much more. That, for us, was a big hit about we've got to live for each moment.

Changes in your basic values and perspectives may seem necessary and desirable, but they also can challenge you individually and as a couple. You and your spouse may not change in the same way, and you may not have the same idea of what a change implies. For example, what if Ted and his wife had different ideas about how to live for each moment? Also, those changes, like the death and your grieving, will make you different from many people around you. That may mean you pull away from relatives and friends or they pull away from you. That throws you and your spouse together more than in the past, just at a time when you are not likely to be at your best in relating to each other.

Will We Divorce?

Many grieving parents are aware of the old research studies that say the divorce rate is much higher for couples who have had a child die, but few parents have heard that those studies are widely criticized by experts or know about other studies that suggest the divorce rate is no higher if a child dies. Although I believe divorce is not necessarily more likely after a child's death, I also understand why couples find it easy to believe that they are more likely to divorce. After a child's death, many couples feel how fragile their marital relationship is, that it is so shaky they could divorce.

Many couples go through very difficult times in their relationship after a child dies, often dealing with difficult marital problems connected to the death for years afterward. There are couples living together like strangers, perhaps even less courteously than strangers. There are couples who stay married despite enormous amounts of anger because one blames the other for the death or cannot forgive the other for grieving the way she or he grieves. Some couples who remain together grow so distant from their partner that it is like an emotional divorce.

Lisa: I can live in the same house with him and not talk to him for a week. Not look at him. It's like a wall between us. And as many times I'm sure *he* thought of just, "Let's get out of this." (*Nick:* I'd thought about it hundreds of times.)

* * * * *

Karl: When Ruth died, we withdrew from everyone, and it was like when Joel died we almost withdrew from each other. It was that little bit deeper, and I love Kathy as much now as I did then, but sometimes I find (crying) that (she's crying too) I just back away. We both go our separate lives.

Kathy: I remember getting into my car every day, crying all the way to work, then getting to work and working, getting in my car and crying all the way home, and taking care of our surviving child, and when I was alone crying again for I don't know how long. And I don't remember Karl in the picture at all.

Karl: And that was obvious. (*Kathy:* Yeah) That's the way I felt, that I wasn't in the picture.

The psychological distance between bereaved partners still together can continue for years. Karl and Kathy still were struggling 12 years after the more recent death.

Karl: You're almost like a roommate now. (*Kathy:* Yeah) That's been pretty much the way our life is now. She'll be sitting at the table, and I'll walk in the door, and unless it's a very, very special occasion it's just, "Hi."

Even if statistics now convince the experts that divorce is not more common for couples who have a child die, some couples who divorce will believe that the death led to the divorce. And many couples who stay together will experience months or years of emotional distance, sexual distance, anger, blaming, and limited communication related to the child dying.

This book is written to help you find ways to head off, minimize, live with, or get past the hard times that you may have together. I have to tell you that I am not against divorce. I think it can be the right choice for one or both partners. But I am also not for divorce. I know that people who think they will or should divorce often can be helped to get to a relationship that is comfortable, affirming, understanding, and loving. Divorce is a way to solve some problems, but often those problems can be solved in other ways.

Grieving Is a Shared Journey

Most of what has been written about grief has focused on individuals, and grief is usually understood and explained as an individual experience. Grieving parents are pushed to think that dealing with a death is basically an individual matter. Yet a grieving couple is so mutually entangled that each is crucial to how the other deals with the death. Grief for a couple whose child has died is very much a couple thing.

Most bereaved parents who are married work out together how to think about the death, how to talk about it, what to believe about it, and how to grieve it. If you are like most married parents, it is your spouse–not somebody else–who most often sees you grieve, who has the most opportunity to understand what you are thinking and feeling in your grief, and who most influences when and how you express and deal with your sorrow. It is with your spouse that you are most likely to figure things out and organize to move ahead.

When a child dies, partners share the loss. You and your spouse had similar relationships to the child, and each of you witnessed the other's relationship with the child. Each of you is likely to be the adult who best knows the other. You probably made many joint decisions concerning the child– including medical treatment, the funeral, and what to do with the child's things. And those decisions will show up in what you think and feel as you grieve. If you are a couple who might have another child, you must decide together whether to do so. In terms of hours per day, each of you may be the adult the other spends the most time with. If you do not deal with your couple issues well enough, your rela- tionship will be in jeopardy, and the end of the marriage can be another devastating loss.

Dealing wisely with your relationship will help head off or minimize difficulties. If you can work together on your relationship, you may have success at backing away from bickering, blaming, and hurt feelings. You may have success dealing with communication difficulties, disappointments, and other issues that can undermine your relationship. And you may be able to offer support, help, and understanding for each other.

Parenting together is a shared journey, and dealing with a child's death is as well. In bereavement, the couple jour- ney will be hard. But it does not have to end in disaster. This book is filled with stories and insights that can help you and your spouse find your way together through the difficulties. It addresses many of the hard issues that come up for bereaved couples, including communication, sexuality, blaming, and whether to use counseling or a support group. This book is not a guide to the one best path; you two have to find your own way. But the information here can encour- age, support, and inspire as you together find your way.

If you want to understand your own or your partner's indi- vidual grief, this book will help, but there are many other books that focus much more on individual grieving. This book focuses on couples. It does not have to be read by a couple to be helpful, though if you both are on the same page and thinking the same things, that might make the book more useful. I know, however, that one spouse typically will read more than the other and that one tries harder than the other to make use of what is read. So do not be surprised if this book is primarily yours or primarily your partner's and not a fully shared resource. But regardless of whether both of you closely read this work, it can still be a couple resource.

2

Deciding to Survive
as a Couple

"We Can't Let This Destroy Us"

AFTER A CHILD'S DEATH, most couples worry that it will be very hard to stay together, and even if they do they often worry about whether they will be able to have a good marital relationship.

Making the Commitment to Stay with Your Partner

If either of you is worried about your marital future, it may help a lot to say to each other that you have those worries and to resolve to stay together. Whether you talk about it immediately or later, it can be an important step toward a strong and lasting relationship. Many grieving parents remember clearly the talk they had with their partner in which they said something like, "It's going to be hard for us, but I am committed to staying with you."

> *Erika:* One thing we talked about the morning we found David dead was we knew that people had problems with marriages after a child died. We made a decision that we were going to continue to be married and that we were going to have to work at it for the other

two children. I didn't want David to be ashamed of us.
We had to do that for his memory, too. I didn't want him
to be the cause of our marriage breaking up.

* * * * *

Elaine: I can remember laying there that night and
thinking that if I could just go to sleep and sleep for a
year I know things would be better then. And I can
remember that night too, him and I laying there and
just making a vow to each other that it would not tear
us apart, because so many people, their family cannot
survive. We held on tight and just decided that we can't,
we just can't let this destroy us.

I think bereaved couples have the same reasons most couples have for staying together–their history together, the ways
they are compatible, the emotional investments their relationship represents, the ways they depend on each other, and
feelings of affection. But I also believe many bereaved parents
are motivated by an additional factor when they make the
commitment to stay together. Their commitment is rooted in
a sense that no one else knew the child as well or could
understand as much what was lost when the child died.

Jane: People seemed to be understanding, but
nobody knew Adam but Rob. And *my* feeling was, and
I was just more and more reinforced in that, *no*body
was gonna be able to understand about the depth of our
loss except this other person who had lived with him.
Not that I was ever *thinking* of leaving or becoming
friendly with anyone else, but I kept thinking, "There's
no one in this world that understands what we've been
through except each other." And I found that as a kind
of a binding thing, a commonality, that more than ever
I felt we had something in common. Not just kids and

a house and a marriage, but the fact that we really understood what we were missing.

Communicating Well and Accepting Differences

With your marriage seeming to be in danger and with the two of you determined to stay together, there will come times when you may want to make resolutions together about ways to keep your relationship strong. One important thing many couples do is resolve to communicate fully and respectfully. Another is to resolve to accept their differences and to accept that they cannot be there for one another all the time.

> **Brett:** After he died, we made a vow that we'd stick together and we would work together, and through the grief group we found out that we grieve differently. And we did. Then we realized that we couldn't help each other at times. And people kept saying, "You have to be there for your wife or your kids."
>
> **Joan:** Sometimes it's just better to be left alone. (**Brett:** Yeah.) Let each other grieve how we need to.
>
> **Brett:** We were one of the few couples that we made a commitment when we knew that there was a problem, that we were gonna work together. As a couple we could decide that we could work toward somethin', and that our love for each other came first, and that these other things were secondary, that we had to maintain our marriage. It wasn't something that was just goin' to take care of itself.

Different Couples, Different Journeys

There is no single path that couples who do well together follow. There is no formula, no sure series of steps that will guarantee a good outcome. Each couple starts at a different place, has different problems to deal with, has different resources available, and brings different histories (including different past experiences with death and other losses), different values, and different personalities to the situation. So each journey is unique.

Some couples have no serious problems after their child's death. But other couples, even years later, struggle to build a comfortable, connecting relationship. Many couples develop a stronger and deeper relationship. Rather than tearing them apart, the loss sets them on a path that brings them closer.

Amy: I think it cemented our relationship a lot stronger.

Ted: You have another common bind together. (*Amy:* Yeah.) You're going through all these things and nobody else understands, and it cements you. It takes you to a different level of knowing that person in just going through that experience together.

Amy: And that made us closer (*Ted:* yeah), made the marriage closer. But don't think that it was all rosy.

* * * * *

Stan: I think it brought us closer together, spiritually. I think it brought us closer together, maybe not taking each other for granted? Like you never know when something is going to happen, so we try to make the most of the time you have together.

* * * * *

Chad: I think we've gotten closer, Erika and I.

Erika: I think it's a different level of intimacy than we've ever had before.

* * * * *

Brett: It actually strengthened our marriage, and it made me a better dad, losing a child. More involved, and I know what's more important as far as money and career and stuff like that. This whole thing strengthened our marriage.

The Luggage You Bring on the Journey

Previous Experiences with Death

As bereaved parents, you travel with luggage from your past. Included in that luggage are your previous experiences, as individuals and as a couple, with death and grief. Such experiences can be a source of problems if, for example, your child's death opens up new and difficult matters concerning a previous death. But experience with death also will give you knowledge and emotional resources to use in dealing with your child's death.

Joan: I don't know if it was easier for me because I'd already been through a lot of death. Brett had never had *any*one die (snorts). And here *I* was with practically everyone I came in contact with. And I don't know if that made it easier. I had a hard time the first year, the first couple of years; it goes in spurts. I don't understand why I could deal with it as well as I did. When my brother committed suicide, I rushed the grieving part, because Alex was still in the hospital. I always thought, "Well why did he do this? How could he do this? What a dumb thing to do. I just talked to him a couple of weeks ago." But then I kind of forgot about it and put all my attentions on Alex. Going through all this death before, I know that eventually things sort of look brighter. And we're not gonna be depressed and have those deep, deep grief feelings for the rest of your life. It slowly starts to lift. Going through all those deaths, I think did help with Alex.

If you or your spouse have never dealt with a major death before, some things are likely to be harder. A first death can produce painful struggles not only with the death but with your own mortality, God's will, how and when to control emotions, whether to ask for help, what a funeral involves, how to deal with the legal and insurance matters, and many other issues. All this can make the pain and confusion of bereavement more challenging.

It also is true that a child's death can be so uniquely painful that there are real limits to how much experience can help. Even if you have dealt with the death of others who were very important in your life, you may never have dealt with feelings as deep and powerful or confusion as profound as you have experienced with your child's death.

Your Shared History Is Likely to Be a Strength

Your history as a couple can be a strength. No matter how old you were when you got together, you have done some growing up together. You have shared many important experiences and come to fit together through years of relationship and shared struggle.

Glenda: We have been married what? Thirty-four and a half years, and I was seventeen and he was eighteen when we got married. We came from strong but stoic backgrounds, and the belief in family and in church, and in hard work, and I think we kept doing most of those things through this, and we did a lot of struggling economically to get Ken through school, and having whole bunches of kids, and I was quite sick, and I think those things forged a good character that helped us through this.

If you are like many couples, your history together gives you many strengths. One of the biggest is you will have developed patterns of dealing together with difficulty, and you automatically will bring those patterns to bear on the immense difficulties connected to your child's death.

> *Glenda:* I think we're both pretty much optimists. I don't think we're pessimistic by nature. And so we kind of force ourselves to look for good. He had a real hard, hard life growing up as far as economics, and mine wasn't too much better. And I grew up in a house of ill-health. I had it modeled for me with my grandfather's Parkinson's disease. My folks took care of him, and lived with my grandparents and my brother and me. Then my dad had a massive heart attack, and from the time I was thirteen my dad was sick for twenty years. So I saw two good role models, my mother and my grandmother. They did what they had to do. And they took care of the sick ones, and they stood by them, and they stood by each other, and didn't walk away from trouble. And you work; and we were both raised to work. You don't have to clean your junk drawer (laughs), but you have obligations.

When Shared History Is Not So Helpful

A couple's history together also can make them vulnerable to problems following the death of their child. If you have lived together for years with intense anger at one another, chronically hurt feelings, communication problems that make almost every day of your relationship together very hard, and frequent doubts about your partnership, you lack a very solid foundation on which to work together after your child dies. I am not talking here about the ordinary squabbles, anger, and frustrations of married life, but about grinding day-after-day difficulties.

> *Earl:* Molly and I right straight up front, we were never really friends. We didn't know each other; we just jumped into marriage. [The couple had divorced.]
>
> * * * * *
>
> *Paul:* Were there other areas of life where your wife was upset?
>
> *Bill:* Oh, oh, man, oh (he laughs). Yeah. It didn't just come about as a result of Steve's death, no. [The couple was divorcing.]

For some couples with a long history of relationship difficulties, the child's death intensifies the problems. If they squabbled before, they argue more often and more bitterly afterward. If there was already considerable anger in the marriage, the child's death intensifies those feelings.

> *Bill:* She's always felt (voice shaking) some anger at me, but more so as a result of this. She said I just didn't *grieve enough* or in the sense that she felt was appropriate. When we get in discussion with it, there were hostilities that would come out that we just couldn't discuss to a point of any resolution to it. [He and his wife were divorcing.]

Sometimes a child's death undermines a couple's patterns of dealing with difficulty, particularly if the child was crucial in keeping the relationship going.

> *Al:* The biggest reason I think that people part after a death like that is that you have the problem finding a reason to go on, to keep going.

Barb: Well you're looking for something.

Al: If you've got the kid, you've got something in common. If he ain't there any longer, well, you've lost that, the bond between the two of you, tying you together. That's what I think is the biggest thing.

If you are a couple who relied on the child to link you, it certainly is possible to forge or discover new links or to find new ways to continue to have the child be a major link. But you also should understand that in being patient with the shared grief process, you need to be patient with the slow and unpredictable process of coming up with new or stronger ties.

Conclusion

For some couples, serious difficulties never arise in dealing with a child's death. But for others, there are real struggles. If you are such a couple, you should know that many marriages survive those difficulties–even those that had problems before a child's death. People learn and change. You can find resources in yourselves and outside that transform you and your marital relationship. Together you can make your marriage work.

3

How a Person Grieves

FOR YOU AND YOUR SPOUSE to get along as a grieving couple, it helps to have a basic understanding of grief. I
think one way grieving spouses get in trouble with each
other is that they do not understand much about grief. Sometimes that means that they have unrealistic expectations for
themselves or their partner. I hope what follows in this chapter will help.

Grief Feelings Are Complicated and Changing

The feelings that come with a death are complicated and
differ from day to day, even moment to moment.

> *Amy:* There are incredible ups and downs that can
> all happen in just a five-minute span. It's not just a good
> day or bad day, it's a good moment; cherish those
> moments.

At any specific moment, grief can involve a mixture of
feelings—for example, a blend of sorrow, rage, helplessness,
anxiety, guilt about outliving your child, physical discomfort,
trouble sleeping, swings in appetite, and self-blame. Sometimes the sad, angry, "down" feelings are blended with the
upbeat feelings—relief, for example, that a life filled with pain

21

has ended or delight at some memory. In fact, almost any conceivable feeling can be part of parental bereavement. There are no "right" or "wrong" feelings.

Because of this complexity, it can be difficult for your spouse or anyone to understand fully what you are feeling. Even if you are both grieving, it is unlikely that your spouse feels exactly the same thing you do at the same time. If you expect to have the same emotions, you might wonder whether something is wrong with you or your spouse. But differences are perfectly normal.

If you feel concerned about not having the same feelings, you might find more similarities in other areas. It is much more likely that you eventually will agree on important elements of your shared story about the child's life, dying, and death and about your relationship, so do not despair about differences in feelings as you go through the grieving process. What you ultimately think and remember probably will be substantially similar.

Another thing about grief is that its intensity can frighten or put off people. Many people do not want to be around someone feeling deep sorrow, rage, anxiety, or depression. They may fear that they will be sucked into feelings they do not want. They may fear that a grieving person may ask too much from them. They can feel discomfort that they do not know what to do or say or that nothing they can do or say can stop those feelings. That means one consequence of normal grieving is that you and your spouse may find yourselves thrown together more, simply because many people slide away from you. (I discuss this more in chapter 9.)

Thinking

To understand how your grief and your partner's play out in your couple relationship, it is important to understand how the death affects your individual thinking. In grieving, especially early on, your thoughts and your partner's return again and again to your child.

Brett: I couldn't stop thinkin' about my son who died. I couldn't work.

* * * * *

George: I was pretty much like a zombie in the inside. Where it's just every thought, no matter what I was doing, like I was eating a meal or watching TV, (*Steph:* mind wandered) wandered. For about a year it was just there *all* of the time.

Steph: I remember driving and looking at beautiful trees and saying, "I shouldn't be looking at these, because our son is never going to see them again."

Your dreams, too, may come back again and again to the death.

Steph: I dreamed that funeral over and over for him (voice shaking). I could tell you what everybody wore.

Some parents repeatedly do a kind of mental searching for the child.

Al: I keep looking up to see that motorcycle coming. And I know it shouldn't, but I keep looking for somebody to come, and there's nobody to come.

Many parents repeatedly review events of the death with a lot of "what ifs." "What if I had done something different? What if we had gotten the child to the hospital sooner?"

Often parents say that for a while they cannot concentrate or think clearly. Focusing so much on the loss (and also being emotionally exhausted and perhaps not getting enough sleep) they might not remember why they picked up the phone, what they were going to talk about with their spouse, or even the sequence of steps in preparing a meal.

Joan: It's very hard to concentrate after that's happened. It's *very* hard to pull all the loose ends together. I was still the food preparer. And I can remember for a long time I could make a salad, or I could make a main course, or I could make a dessert. But I could hardly *ever* make a salad and a dessert and a main course. I just *could*n't pull all three of 'em together.

For weeks, months, or even longer, a child's death strips daily activities to the basics.

Gabe: You just do what's in front of you.
Sue: Keep showing up.

Doing only the basics can mean that preventive maintenance on the car, house, or marriage is overlooked. With so much of your thinking focussed on the child, things that sustain your couple relationship–such as planning together or going for walks–are neglected. When these things are lost, it can seem the couple relationship is fading. Small wonder that your thoughts in grief may be not only about the death or the "what ifs," but also about what has happened to your marriage.

Also in grief, your thoughts may return again and again to concerns that your spouse or a surviving child could die and that your emotional vulnerability to additional loss is enormous.

Your Child's Death Brings Many Losses

A child's death involves many different losses for a parent. Some are apparent immediately, and some you will only begin to experience days, weeks, months, or even years later.

Louise: You go through not so much the loss of a child but the loss*es*, like he would've graduated. This would have been his second year of college. What would he be doing? Pretty soon his friends are gonna start getting married. They'll have children. What would he have looked like as an adult?

Wayne: You aren't going to be going in the same circles anymore, (*Louise:* No) because Will was the bond of going in the circles.

* * * * *

Denny: I would have gotten to read to him, and play catch with him, teach him to swim, and see him with his mom. Every dream we have is gone. You come back to an empty house and an empty nursery, and people don't know what to say.

* * * * *

Joy: We always figure your daughter is going to grow up and she'll be your friend, and you'll go shopping together, and you'll eat lunch. I just hoped Jenny would grow up to be a real wholesome Christian young woman, with good values, and ultimately grow up and be a mom, and I'd help her with her kids, and I'd go over and cook dinner for her (laughing) so she could have a break. One thing I know that Stan was really sad about was that she'd never have kids, and he'd never be a grandpa for her kids.

New developments in your life can bring new losses related to your child's absence.

Joy: Our two children born after she died were like seventeen months apart, and there were days when I'd be so overwhelmed I'd stand at the kitchen sink and both these kids in diapers and tears would be coming down my face. It's like "Jenny, I need you here." She would have been like fifteen or fourteen, and I could just imagine that she'd be helping me so much with the little kids. When the babies were little, I felt a real loss, not only for her help but for what she was missing. She would have been so excited to have these babies. A couple of my friends had their babies right before the accident, and she asked me, "Mom, when are we going to have our baby?"

Important achievements or seemingly positive changes in the family can be grieved because the child who died is not present to witness or participate in them.

Some parents grieve for the memories of their child that fade away.

> *Glenda:* I can't hear his voice anymore. I used to be able to hear. I don't know what he sounds like.

Losses that you experience in your marital relationship as a result of the death also are grieved—for example, emotional intimacy, lighthearted conversation, or sexual intimacy.

Different Time Course for Different Loss Feelings

Sometimes a specific aspect of the loss is felt intensely, but then things happen that reduce or eliminate that feeling. Parents do not "get over" a child's death, but they may get past the pain of specific aspects of loss associated with the death.

With each of the many aspects of loss you experience having a different time frame, switching from one thought about the death to another may produce very different feelings. You may be at peace about not being able to save your daughter or son from pain, but you may still be grieving intensely the loss of the grandchildren that child might have brought into your life. It also means that you can feel at peace with the death at one moment and have very strong feelings again at another. Those swings may come as a surprise to both you and your spouse.

Different People Experience Different Losses

Different people experience different losses. One partner, for example, may grieve the loss of descendants but not think at all about losing the sound of the child singing, but the other partner may feel strong grief about missing the child's singing while not caring about descendants. So even though you and your spouse share many feelings associated with the death of the child, you also will, to some extent, be grieving for different losses.

Grief Keeps Bubbling Up

Although some people say grieving takes a specific amount of time, the period they suggest usually is much shorter than what most grieving parents experience. For a child's death, grief often lasts a lifetime. Yes, a lifetime. Those feelings may become less intense or less often intense, and they may be less often present after a number of years, but for many parents the grieving never comes to an end.

Gabe: There's always the sting. You always feel it. It always colors your thinking. [His daughter died thirty-two years ago.]

* * * * *

Joan: It goes in spurts, like last year on his (*Brett:* anniversary) anniversary of his death I was having a real hard time. It was because he was five years old. It's not anything that's every year the same time. Some Christmases I have a hard time and some I don't.

* * * * *

Bonnie: You never know when it's going to hit. I can be just fine, not even think about it, and somebody will say something, and I just get over*whelmed.*

* * * * *

Chad: You think about him all the time, not constantly, but there's just little reminders no matter where you go.

Erika: Sometimes they bring tears, and sometimes we laugh.

Although most parents do not grieve constantly after the intense initial period of mourning, reminders of the loss that crop up can bring back the grieving. The most common include almost anything about children (TV commercials with children, children at the grocery store, children in a playground) and almost anything dealing with death and grief. They also include the first return to places somehow connected to the child (for example, a doctor's office), activities (for example, shopping for children's clothing, talking with someone who knew the child), dates connected to the child (particularly anniversaries of the child's birth and death), and holidays.

For some parents, it is not only that a holiday can be filled with painful reminders, but also that other people, even those who know better, may try to act as though nothing has changed, creating an even more painful sense of loss (the loss of support or acknowledgement or shared feelings).

Television might be used to distance feelings of grief, but it also can provide potent reminders.

Brett: I have a hard time watching television when a kid is sick. (chuckling) I always tear up.

* * * * *

Earl: There's not a TV program that I can watch if it's got children in it or if there's some sad scene in it that doesn't make me think of my children who died, seeing youngsters on TV and playing some sport or something, and it makes me cry. I can't watch the Olympics because of all the youngsters on there.

Places also can bring up memories, And parents sometimes avoid or even flee places that are painful reminders.

Louise: You'd be in a store and you'd see something (*Wayne:* Set you off, something that you recognize that David used to go to). Right, yeah, I remember I couldn't go into the grocery store for probably two years afterwards, because he always went with me shopping, and you'd be in a grocery store and all of sudden you'd see something and you'd almost take it off the shelves, and then you'd realize I'm buying this for David, and he doesn't exist anymore. Then I'd just leave the cart. I left a lot (*Wayne:* Yeah, yeah) of grocery carts. I'd get *horrible* panic attacks in stores, and I had to leave. I couldn't breathe.

Children who are like the child while he or she was alive or who are the age the child would be can be sharp reminders of the loss as well.

Amy: Every time I see a five-month-old baby, that does something to me.

* * * * *

Joy: There's people that are friends of ours that have girls that are around Jenny's age, and I really feel the loss when they're here, and it's like if only Jenny were here, they'd be such good friends. In Sunday school, we were helping a dance class, and there was a little girl that just absolutely reminded me of Jenny in the way she was sitting and cutting and drawing. And I just couldn't handle it. I had to leave the Sunday school room, because I was just sobbing.

* * * * *

Marsha: Denny's sister had her baby four days after Matt's funeral, and she had a little boy. He's our godson, and we've been watching him grow up. (*Denny:* One-year birthday party), yeah, we had to go through all that, which has been tough, and we love him dearly, but it's been hard.

Denny: Christmas he's dressed up in Santa Claus stuff, and I'll go look at him in his playpen and start bawling. And my sister comes in and hugs me.

Marsha: The emotions that you go through, you're so happy for her, but yet (*Denny:* You're jealous. Just flat out jealous).

Things around the house will also be reminders.

Al: We have welders in the shop, torches. I taught him how to use them all. You go back down and start working that stuff and see things he's made and tools he was using, takes you a long time to put that away (voice cracks).

Communications that come after the child died based on the assumption that the child is still alive are painful reminders.

Kathy: You get the calls and being a new mother, and all the people are soliciting things, and calling you on the one year birthday of your child, and you get things in the mail, and this went on for a long time, and just kinda adds salt to the wound.

* * * * *

Barb: He had decided to do the Air Force, and he went down and took the physical. The Air Force signer-upper came to the funeral. He knew Tom had been killed. A month after that the phone rang, "Is Tom there?" I thought what in the hell is going on now? And I said, "No, he isn't!" Well when could he get a hold of him? And I said, "I am sorry, but he was killed a short while ago. Who is this?" Well this was the Air Force recruitment office. I said, "Is this [name of the recruiter who was at the funeral]?" "No, he's not here anymore." And I said, "My God, look in your records!" And I just hung the phone up. And then we had a thing come when Tom would have turned eighteen. They sent us a three-page form [asking] why he thought he was exempted from joining the armed forces. And they had a phone number, so I called and said that he had been killed. That was just too bad. We had to send obituary, death certificate, proof that he was killed. I said, "My God, lady, do you think I'd stand here and tell you that?"

Some women, particularly if they have lost an infant or young child, say that somebody else's pregnancy, giving birth, or being with a young child can be a painful reminder.

Sally: My sisters-in-law on both sides of the family had children. It caused me such pain to have them come to town with their children, to brag about their children, to complain about their children. I used to hate pregnant women.

* * * * *

Tina: One day I opened up this card [from friends of ours] and here it was a birth announcement. They'd had a baby girl. And I remember saying, "Oh, *God!* They had a baby girl." And Scott said, "That's *terr*ible. They've been trying for years to have a baby." And I felt bad, because I really hurt inside, 'cause I wanted, *I* wanted to have a baby. Or if people would invite me to a baby shower, it's like, (sounding amused and horrified at something ridiculous) "I can't go to a baby shower." "Oh come on. It'll be fun." And again, they didn't mean to be hurtful, but it cut me the wrong way.

* * * * *

Molly: I went to church and it was very difficult for me to see the other moms with their kids. I remember leaving many times, not being able to deal with it.

Others may say things that remind you of the death, sometimes because they have themselves been reminded of the death.

Stan: Our older son would bring things up, "Hey, this is what Jenny did." And then you'd remember (laughs) and know that she can't do it anymore, or at least not here.

Wanting to Remember

Many parents say that they feel that they cannot, should not, and must not let go of their grief and that they must not forget their child. Thus, even though reminders of the child can be painful, grieving parents do not necessarily avoid the reminders, nor do they try to change their thinking so the reminders will become less significant.

Family members, friends, and coworkers may not understand the attraction of reminders and the desire of bereaved parents to continue to remember the child and to feel the child's loss. So they may try to avoid talking about the child or putting the parents in situations where they are reminded of the loss. Many parents are clear that they much prefer talking about the child and facing possibly painful reminders of the child than not.

> *Stan:* You just want to talk about it, and a lot of people don't want to talk about it.
>
> *Joy:* Yeah, I talk to a lot of people still about Jenny. And I think a lot of people don't want to bring it up because they feel like they'll hurt your feelings, and I've told them, "You know what? It hurts my feelings more when you don't talk about her." Because I haven't forgotten about her, and your talking about her isn't going to, "Oh gosh. I had forgotten all about Jenny until you mentioned her."

You or your spouse may at times want to avoid or ignore reminders in order to get some emotional balance, but at other times one of you may seek them out, even if they are painful.

Spouses Differ in What Is a Painful Reminder

Another common difference between spouses is that whether or how much a thing or place is a painful reminder can vary. For example, one spouse may have strong reactions to the school their child attended, while the other spouse has little or no reaction at all.

Having Much Less Energy Than Before

It is common while grieving to have much less energy than before, and sometimes a bereaved parent does the bare minimum of daily activities only if somebody else pushes, prods, and helps.

> *Gail:* My girlfriend came over. After the funeral, we were home for two or three days. And then he went back to work. And I remember getting up in the morning, the kids would get up, and we'd all sit around (chuckling) in our pajamas until she came and said, "Now it's time to take a shower and get dressed (chuckles), and we'll eat." And we went, "Okay." She came over like every other day for a month. And she'd bring a hot dish or something, and say, "Okay, now it's time to go take a shower. You dress." She got the kids dressed. She was a lifesaver.

Having the energy to do more than the bare minimum, such as planning and taking a vacation, does not come easily. But when it does, it is a symbol of having made real progress in dealing with the death.

> *Iris:* When Jeff was sick in the hospital, we had decided that if he died we were gonna go to Hawaii, to take a vacation to relax and recover. And when he did die, we didn't have the energy to do that. And we didn't want to ruin a perfectly nice trip, and we ended up waiting about a year. And it seemed like Todd couldn't make any plans beyond his nose, where he'd never been that way before. He's always been a planner and this and this and this and this and this, *way* down the road. After [Jeff] died, Todd couldn't seem to shake himself out of that, and when we finally started talking about going to Hawaii again, he couldn't decide, should we or shouldn't we. And finally he decided we will do it, and to me it seemed like that was a *big* milestone for us.

Greater energy will come with time. I do not know if this will work for you, but sometimes energy might be recovered for a while by acting as though you have energy. For example, some couples talk about feeling as if they do not want to do something (say, visit friends or go to a movie) but then find that once they get into it they feel more energized.

Developing a Story of the Death and Its Aftermath

In coming to terms with a child's death, each parent travels his or her own individual path. For many parents, an important part of coming to terms with what happened is to become clear about the events leading up to the death, the death, and what happened afterward. The story the parent eventually has in mind and may tell to others often is quite detailed. As part of the process of getting to that story, there will be considerable time and energy devoted to thinking through the details, remembering exactly what happened when, and trying to fill in the gaps.

If you listened with me to other parents telling their stories, it would be obvious that their stories always cover events leading up to the death and the death itself. Their stories almost always emphasize how special the child was, not only for the parents but also for others. A lot of the stories you would hear include a discussion of whether something could have been done to prevent or delay the death. So their stories are partly about personal efforts or personal helplessness, what they tried, why they couldn't do more, and how much was in the hands of others (for example, doctors, sheriff deputies, or paramedics). Lots of parent stories also are about responsibility and blame for the death.

I have puzzled about why so many parents blame themselves or their partner, even when it seems that, for most couples, they made no choice that they could have known would result in their child's dying. My guess is that it is a way of saying life is not completely out of control. "Things my partner and I can do can make a difference—obviously for bad, but hopefully for good." I think in that sense blaming is a part of healing. It says, "We have the power to make a difference." Also, it seems to be part of healing or coming to terms with a death for many bereaved parents to eventually back away from blaming— themselves, their partner, God, or anyone or anything else. The story may still deal to some extent with blame and responsibility, but blame becomes a less significant part of the story.

Clearing Up Relations with God

Many bereaved parents struggle with what God was up to when a child died. In their anger, confusion, or anxiety about God, it is common for parents to struggle with questions of whether there is a God, whether God is good, whether God is just, why God let the death happen, or why God took that child at that time.

> *Hannah:* I took care of my husband's mom when she was dying. I did it because I thought that was my place to be. And to this day I have a hard time not being angry with God, because I keep thinking I did what I thought was best, and I probably was a pretty good person, and then my reward is He takes my kid away. I still don't understand that.

*   *   *   *   *

Amy: I think because of all of the deaths that have been close to me, my mother and my son and my brother and some other things that have happened, it's *real* hard to see the goodness in God.

Some parents feel that God has made something happen that is more than they could or should handle.

Hannah: I did not think that I would ever survive this. Everybody has their limits. That's why people say (imitating an unintelligent, busybody voice:) "God never gives you more than you can handle." Well, will somebody get a message through to Him that I've had enough.

Stages or Not?

Some grief experts say bereaved people go through a series of stages, while others disagree with that view. Similarly, some bereaved parents believe there are stages of grief and some do not. Among those who believe in stages, some think there is a predictable progression, and some, like the woman quoted below, feel that one could move back and forth among the stages.

Kelly: We know that we will be going through these stages, again and again. And we can bounce into one stage, into another stage.

In trying to understand your grief or your spouse's, one of you may believe in stages and one not, one of you may seem to grieve in orderly stages and one not. My opinion is that thinking in terms of stages really helps some people and makes trouble for others. The trouble might include feeling bad about oneself or partner if the grieving does not seem to fit what is believed to be the proper pattern. So I am not going to tell you that your grief and your spouse's will go through a set of predictable stages, but if it seems to and that feels right, I am glad that way of looking at grief works for you.

Sense of Presence

"Sense of presence" refers to the experience of feeling in contact with a person who died. For bereaved parents, the experiences range from a sense of spiritual contact with the child, a sense that even though the child cannot be seen or heard the child is present, to vivid experiences of hearing and seeing the child.

> *Chad:* The morning after he died, I'm sitting here, hadn't slept all night, looked out, and just as clear as could be I could see him standing right there at the corner. He walked toward my office, by the barn, and he had a kind of a slow pigeon-toed shuffle, just turned around and looked. And then he went one more step around the edge of the barn (bangs on table), shuffled along kind of slow (his voice cracks) and a little bit pigeon-toed, just there he was.
>
> *Erika:* (bangs the table) I wished I would've seen it. I believe the spirit stays with you for a while. I think he was here for a while.

Some parents have sense of presence experiences that are intensely spiritual but that also lead them to question their sanity.

> *Lisa:* I don't know how to start this one. I myself believe I have (sounding embarrassed), if I'm not

wacko, some kind of psychic powers (embarrassed laugh). Or, when something happens (snap of fingers) a bell goes off in my head, like it was right after Craig died. I used to always tell him, "Now turn the light off." So he'd sit there and he'd switch the thing on and off. What happens right after he died? That front light over there, I went to turn it off, wouldn't go off. I just sat there and flicked it on and off, and it was like, "Oh, my God. This is Craig doing that." I have sensed that he's peaceful.

To the extent that people connect sense of presence with a place—that the spirit of a child who died stays near where the child lived or where the child died—places can be very important to parents. One woman talked about why she and her husband did not want to sell the house where their son had died.

Erika: He'd lived here with us. We had happy times here, and more importantly he did die here. And so that threshold (she bangs on table six times) that he crossed over into death was *here* (she bangs on the table once). I can stand in the same spot he stood in. This was the spot.

Conclusion

I have tried with this discussion of individual grief to provide a sense of what you and your spouse have been going through and will go through. One major thing to remember is that there is an enormous range and complexity to grieving and that everyone grieves differently. A second major thing to remember is that you and your spouse will differ in how you grieve, what you grieve, and the timing of your grief. A big part of understanding grief and of getting along as a couple is to understand and accept that the two of you are unlikely to grieve about the same things in the same ways at the same times. You probably will agree about many important things, but you are quite likely to differ in what you feel and when you feel it.

4

Two People Always
Grieve Differently

YOU AND YOUR SPOUSE will not grieve the same
way. You differ in biology, personality, upbringing, current
responsibilities, the relationship you had with the child, and
life experiences. Even if those things didn't guarantee that
you and your partner will mourn in your own way, women
and men differ in numerous ways that will show up in how
you deal with your child's death.

In some couples, one partner believes how or when the
other grieves is wrong, or one partner's grief makes the other
feel uncomfortable. If, over a long period, you let such differences upset you or if your differences lead to conflict, they
can be a wedge that pushes the two of you far apart.

Fred: My grief is just completely different than hers.
Hers is a mess.

Hannah: You deal with things by running. He goes
on motorcycle trips a lot.

Fred: I've always been that way.

Hannah: I'd rather confront and take care of it right
away, and we've always been different that way. I don't
feel like I got support from Fred right away. When Fred

was ready, I already had the barrier up. And I thought, "I've gotten this far by myself, and I'm not going to allow anybody else (*Fred:* yeah) to get into my grieving."

Fred: It got so bad that she accused me that I didn't put my arm around her, to hold her, to talk to her.

Hannah: But physically you weren't there.

Fred: Oh, yeah, I was there, but she didn't remember me even holding her. You can only reach out so far before you feel pushed away. And it happened. Within the first month it was happening. I was back at work; she wasn't. I wish she'd gone back to work, but she couldn't.

Hannah: And every day when I came home, he would say, "You should be back at work. You shouldn't be sitting in the house."

Fred: Yeah. And see it's a wedge got in there.

A key to getting along, staying together, and going through the grieving process feeling supported by one another is to recognize and accept your differences. Some couples will find a way to see eye to eye on everything and to grieve in similar ways, but that's unusual. The rest of this chapter talks about what I think are the common differences in grieving, and understanding that you are likely to differ in these ways will, I hope, help you to be comfortable with and accepting of your differences.

Timing

Spouses have different paces into and through various parts of grieving. One partner might have stronger feelings or a certain feeling soon after the loss, while the other might feel those things later. To some parents, there seems to be a route to travel, and they talk about being farther or less far along than their partner. When they talk like that, there sometimes is a sense that being farther along is better, perhaps even more moral. But I don't think one pace is better than the other. Feelings of superiority or inferiority about the pace of grieving or the belief one partner's pace is better than the other's will make trouble you don't need. There is no scientific basis for saying one pace in grieving is better than another.

One of you might move quickly into active talking, reading, thinking, and feeling to deal with the death, while the other might not. Again, I think accepting the difference is desirable.

One of you may try to be "strong" while the other is grieving intensely. "Strong" might mean doing necessary things around the house instead of focusing on grief or feeling that there was no point in doing things. "Strong" might mean not being swamped emotionally, or it might mean acting like things will be better. Lots of men feel the need to be strong for their partner, holding off their grief in order to be strong and supportive.

> *Todd:* I felt like I had to be the one to be hopeful, to be strong and steady, and I thought that would be a help to Iris, 'cause she was more emotionally tied in with the baby, as mothers are, not that I wasn't, but the mother always is closer. It was harder for me after the first two years. I think because I felt like I had a duty to be strong for her. So I couldn't let my emotions mess me up so much. Then after she got over it a little more and was (*Iris:* functional [laughs]), yeah, a little more functional, then I kind of relaxed and it caught up with me. The third year was quite a bit harder for me.

* * * * *

Tina: I kind of feel sorry for men, because I think raised in the society that we are, they're not really allowed to express their feelings. And they have to be the strong one.

The differences in grieving common between men and women are driven by the standards and expectations of society, and one way to better understand how society pushes men and women to mourn in distinct ways is to recall how some people interact differently with you and your spouse.

Hannah: They'll come up to Fred and say (in a hearty voice), "How're you doing?" They'll come up to me and say (in a gentle voice), "How are you doing?" At the funeral ceremony, Fred and I were standing there, side by side (*Fred:* yeah). They presented me with the flag. And at that point, I thought, "Why was it me, and why wasn't it his dad that got the flag?" I felt kind of bad for him, because he was a parent to his child. I really felt bad for him that day. At the funeral and at the wake, it seemed like I was never without someone right there at my side, and I looked and Fred was kinda wandering around. And it seems that they always go to the female. I don't know if it's because people perceive the female as needing more comfort. They ask me more sensitive questions than they asked him.

* * * * *

Kathy: With both deaths, people always were asking him how *I* was. He was hurting just as much. But everyone kind of expected him to be real tough. It was okay for me to fall apart (*Karl:* yes), and I knew that he had fallen apart, too.

I don't think of grieving as a sign of weakness and of controlling emotions as a sign of strength, but many grieving parents do. As I see things, grieving can be strong, but it can make one needier and make it harder to do other things, like daily chores. It is common in couples for one partner (more often the man) to stay away from feelings in order to be strong while the other grieves, but that does not mean that strong emotions do not show up months or years later.

If spouses return to work outside the home at different times, the pace of their progress along the path of grieving also can vary. A partner who returns to work soon after the death might take longer to get to certain feelings or thoughts. Going back to work puts pressure on a parent to bottle up feelings and makes it more difficult to find the time to read about grief or use other resources. The work situation draws a parent away from thoughts and feelings about the child, and that can show up in how each spouse deals with the loss and each other. Returning to work soon after the death may delay dealing with certain feelings and thoughts. A partner who continues to stay home may have more freedom to grieve and may make more progress in feeling and thinking about the child's death.

Emotions

Partners almost always differ in the feelings they express or how they show those feelings. Both partners often believe the woman is more expressive or displays emotions in a way easy to label as "sad." Some men are concerned about grieving too little or expressing too little sadness, and are relieved if they find themselves crying and sad.

Differences in outward emotion lead to resentment in some couples. When one spouse feels down and the other seems up, each may resent the other. One might, for example, think "How can you dare to be so upbeat when our child is dead?" While the other might think, "When you are down like this you drag me down," or "Get over it," or "I am worried about you." But such differences are to be expected and, I think, accepted.

Sometimes a difference in emotionality pushes partners not to share much with one another. Perhaps each does not want to be affected by the other, or does not think the other will be understanding, or respects the other's feelings and does not want to offend the other. The upshot is that some grieving parents feel alone when they are feeling more or less emotional than their partner. This type of difference also can lead to feeling something is wrong with oneself.

> *Sue:* I felt lonely. Yeah, and it was because we both handled it differently. And I think I felt like I was probably dysfunctional, that there was something wrong with me that I couldn't look at this in that same kind of a calm way.

Sue could laugh about it decades later, but at the time, the difference was hard for her.

Tears

In many couples, one partner, typically the woman, cries more in grief. The partner who cries less can be uncomfortable with the other's tears, but also may come to be more accepting.

> *Ken:* When she was crying, "I'd say, ptht, you go to sleep." But at least I got to the point, "Let her do what she has to do. Accept that."

* * * * *

Iris: I'd lay in bed and cry at night, and he'd lay over near me and be embarrassed and not know what to do (laughing).

Todd: Yeah, I didn't know exactly how to handle it when she'd be crying, didn't know what I could do to make her feel better. Not that I didn't want to. But I guess I was just at a loss on what to do.

Iris: I think we were very frustrating to each other, because I would speak of all my emotional reactions to things people said, and I'm missing Jeff. And then he'd get upset with me, because he sees it from more of a cerebral point of view.

A child's death leads some men to become more comfortable with their own crying and more likely to cry than they were before. But still, differences in this area can be a big problem.

Earl: Things just kinda worked their way into a unrelationship type thing. Molly didn't understand why I did not cry at first. And I told her that I had to be there for her. I said, "I'll cry, and I do cry, but I'm here to support you." And I've never been forgiven for that, for not crying at the time.

Anger

Anger is common in grieving, and for some people it comes back again and again for years. I still experience anger over the medical malpractice nine years ago that led to my grandson's death. I have even more anger about the coverup at the clinic where the malpractice occurred. They "lost" all his medical records, so it is impossible to know what the attending physician did or did not do.

In some couples one spouse feels and expresses more anger than the other. Most often the anger seems directed at the fact of death, those who were responsible for a fatal accident, a physician, a health maintenance organization, a hospital, people who said offensive things, God, or themselves. Some spouses seem to take turns being angry, and partner differences in anger are to be expected. If you are the more angry one, you might feel mad that your spouse is not angry, but it is very human to find other things to do with feelings than be angry. (For example, my son and daughter-in-law do not share my anger about the medical malpractice and the loss of records.) If you are the less angry one, I think that ordinarily the best thing to do is to acknowledge your partner's feelings and be patient with them. If the anger is directed at you, though, I think working on communication, mutual understanding, apologies (if appropriate), and peacemaking would be important.

Guilt

Many bereaved parents feel guilt. They may feel guilt about the genes they gave the child, choices they made about medical care, the times they felt they were not there for the child, or any of a million other things connected to their child's life and death. They can even feel guilt about feeling happy or enjoying themselves.

In some couples, spouses differ in whether or how much they feel guilt, making it another area that needs to be dealt with through acceptance and an understanding that such differences are normal. I would even say that sometimes a grieving parent needs to feel guilt, and trying to take it away would deprive her or him of something valuable. But I also think that for some people not feeling guilt is almost a religious or spiritual thing, that they do not feel guilt because they have a spiritually grounded belief that the death—like most things in life—was out of their control.

Emotional Control

Most grieving people control their emotions some of the time, for example, so they can be composed in public, to avoid upsetting others, to keep from becoming too depressed, or because they need to focus on tasks that cannot be done if they are feeling certain feelings too strongly. In lots of couples, however, one partner controls emotions more than the other, and typically this is the man.

A difference in emotional control can be a source of discomfort or even resentment.

> *Tina:* I really resented Scott because, and these were his exact words, "Well, I can just put her away in a little package, and if I want to think about her I can take her out, and if I don't want to think about her, she can just be in there." He was at work, too, so he had things to occupy his mind, and here I was at home. But that really bothered me, 'cause I couldn't do that. And I really resented that, and then I felt like he wasn't talking to me about his pain or what he was going through, and he'd make comments like (imitating a confident male voice), "Well, I talked to people at work about it. I have my sadness in the car on the way home, and then when I get home I'm okay, just put her away in this little package."

There can be misunderstanding on both sides. The partner who controls emotions less can resent the other for seeming not to care about the child or acting superior. The partner who controls emotions more may not understand how much the one who is more emotional must be that way.

Neither may grasp that what they see in the other is normal and right.

In some couples there seems to be turn-taking in emotional control. When one partner is deep in grief, the other controls his or her emotions enough to do the basics and perhaps to say things meant to be soothing and supportive.

Talk

Talking with Spouse

In many couples one partner (more often the woman) talks more about the death. The difference can be wearing to both partners.

> *Sue:* He got sick of hearing me. That's what I was feeling. I would talk to him and he was really support-ive when I was going through this stuff, but it gets to be repetitious, and I pretty much did a lot of this on my own.
>
> *Gabe:* I was raised in a time where you just don't talk about these things. So somebody died and you go on.

Spouses may also have trouble talking with each other because one or both want to avoid disagreement, argument, or anger.

> *Fred:* Instead of arguing, I run away. I don't want to be in arguments.
>
> *Hannah:* And you also don't want to hear certain things.
>
> *Fred:* Sure I don't. There's stuff I don't want to hear, and we get into it, and she speaks up, well then I snap away (she laughs). Running away, whatever you want to call it. Yeah, I do.

When one partner is more interested in talking than the other, there is the problem of what to do about the difference.

Rosa: I remember planning, thinking, "Okay, Henry is working hard." I'd spend a half a week planning a picnic. Okay, we'll go to this nice little park, cooking a meal, doing everything, getting the basket, taking everything, going there, laying out the blanket, and meanwhile saying, "He hasn't said a thing all afternoon." Coming home thinking, "I gotta kill him. I gotta kill him." Or when we went out to a friend's cottage and me saying, "You're quiet." You're going, "Well, you want me to relax. I'm relaxed." And really feeling quite rejected. I took it as being rejected.

Henry: Yeah, right. It was all subconscious to me. I wasn't doing it on purpose (*Rosa:* no). I just didn't want to deal with anything.

The one who wants more conversation might decide to wait it out, but might still feel angry that the partner will not talk. Also, just as the spouse who wants to talk finds the other's silence frustrating and infuriating, the spouse who wants to talk less can be irritated by the other's pressure to talk.

Talking with Others

It is common for one spouse to talk less about the death to people in general and to have fewer people with whom to talk.

Stan: Joy had more friends that she could talk to, more close girlfriends. I really didn't have any. I played ball with guys once a week, but I didn't really see 'em besides that. So she really had more of an outlet. She had the chance to talk, and then other people would also have the chance to try to bring her up. Whereas I really didn't have that. I kinda had to do it myself. I wish I had that, especially have had it back then.

Spouses also differ in how likely they are to let strangers know about the death.

> *Joy:* I can talk about Jenny easier than Stan can. Like when people will ask us how many kids we have, I always say five, and he always says four. It's just that I have to validate her, and that's how, and a lot of times I'll just say we have four here and one in heaven, and that's as far as it will go. I can't say four because we have five. It's okay for him to say four, but for me that's just not okay. And I'll give him a little poke when I'm with him and he says four.

In my experience, some men say they have nobody or nobody other than their partner with whom to talk or that virtually all their talk about the death has been with their spouse, whereas I don't think I have ever heard a woman say those things.

Valuing Support Groups

All over the United States, but particularly in urban areas, there are support groups for bereaved people (see chapter 10). Often there are support groups specifically for bereaved parents. Many times, spouses will differ in how much they attend or participate in such groups, and more often it is the woman who wants to attend and is active in one.

> *Lisa:* I went to Compassionate Friends on and off for a couple of years.
> *Paul:* Was it helpful?
> *Lisa:* Oh, yeah. Other people that were there, every one of 'em had lost a child. And just talking, it helps to

talk. He went once. That was I think a year later. He didn't like it.

Nick: I wasn't ready to talk about him. I couldn't. I still, six years I still break down when I talk about it. I was hurtin' too bad, and I didn't know how she could do it. I never understood that. I don't care how many people were there that had kids die. I had one, mine, and I had my own problem. I don't need to listen to ten other people's problems. I was raised to do things by myself. If I ever had a problem, I had to sort it out myself.

If both partners go to a support group, it more often is the man who is reluctant to do so.

Thinking

Many couples differ in how much, when, and what they think about the child who died—especially in how much they think about "what ifs" and why the death happened.

In some couples, spouses hold different beliefs about whether or how they will come to know in heaven why God took their child.

Partners also may differ in how much they can, will, or want to avoid thinking about the child's death.

Brett: I couldn't sleep, and I lost my appetite, and I had a lot of those kinds of problems. She said, "Just don't think about it." I still don't understand how you can just not think about somethin'.

Often one spouse will remember things the other does not, and sometimes one or both can be upset about these differences. One reason is that to some people remembering means caring, so a partner can be upset that the spouse does not remember seemingly important things because it seems to mean the spouse does not care. But the reality is that two people will always differ in how much they pay attention to details, what details they pay attention to, and how easily they can recall memories.

Partners also may differ in how many things remind them of the loss. And sometimes that can be an issue, especially if the one who is more often reminded of the loss feels annoyed that the other is not or if the one who is not reminded believes something is wrong with the partner for feeling reminded (and then emotional).

Partners often differ also in what they think about storing the child's clothing and other possessions and also about moving from the home they were living in when the child died. While one may prefer storing or getting rid of clothing and possessions and moving to another house, the other may think exactly the opposite. This is a difficult issue for some couples, because compromise may seem impossible. If one spouse has it his or her way, the other can experience a sense of loss or anger. Nevertheless, I think even understanding that the difference is real and normal is a big step toward dealing with the problem.

Going to the Cemetery

One partner often is more comfortable going to the cemetery or more inclined to go. The difference is not necessarily a source of conflict, but it can be a source of guilt.

> *Glenda:* I think people think we're functional, but we're pretty dysfunctional (laughing through the tears). And I can't go to the cemetery. My husband goes to the cemetery. I go out there and I collapse on the ground. Then I feel guilty because I can't go to the cemetery.

Sleeping

Grieving spouses differ in how much and how well they sleep. The difference can sometimes be a problem, with frustrations or resentments on either or both sides.

Vince: I remember how *mad* you got at me for going to sleep one night.

Gail: (sounding irritated) That was the day Randy died. We're laying in bed. I'm crying. It's 2:30 a.m., and (bang on table) he is *snoring* like crazy. And I just thought that was horrible. I thought, "How can you sleep? Your kid just died." I could not sleep for months. Just a horrible sleep for months.

Vince: See, I knew I had to get some sleep so that I could hold us up some more.

Gail: I had no idea what was gonna help the next day, that you have to go make funeral arrangements and people would be here and I had to think and function. And the kids would come home. All I could think of was, "Randy's dead. Randy's dead."

Reading

Partners often differ in how much they read about grief. Sometimes the one who reads more resents the other's not wanting to learn from what has been written or not valuing what the reader has to say that comes from reading. Or the one who reads less believes that reading is a way of avoiding problems or that the other uses what is read to criticize or to try to change him or her.

I think typically it is the woman who reads more, whether because feelings are more of a focus for her or because women are more often readers in general. Some men read, but focus on medical or technical matters that can help them to understand what has happened to the child.

Some parents feel that reading will help their partner to understand them better. One woman whose husband thought she was crazy because of how she was grieving wanted her husband to read about grief so he would understand that she was normal.

> *Scott:* I thought I was gonna have to commit her to (laughs) someplace. I was very concerned. I, like other people, thought, well, "Gosh, you should be moving on."
>
> *Tina:* It was like everybody behind my back is sitting and waiting, "When's she gonna finally snap?" I'd be doin' okay, and then *WHAM*, somethin' would happen. And I'd feel like I was back the day it happened. One of those times was when he said, "You're worse now. We're gonna have to do something with you." And (chuckles) I'm thinking, "Jeez! This is great (laughs). All these people are supposed to love and care about me," and I did all kinds of reading about grief and the grieving process and time periods. Part of me knew that, "No, this is all right. This is two, three months after the fact. It's okay."
>
> *Scott:* And I did not. (*Paul:* You didn't read?) No, that was another area of conflict.
>
> *Tina:* He wouldn't even read like a paragraph (laughs).

Physical Effort and Grieving

Sometimes spouses differ in how much they need to be physically active in their grief, for example, to chop wood, lift weights, exert muscles, hit things hard, or run.

Chad: The best thing for me to do was to go out physically do something, physically get something accomplished. And being on a farm, I could do that. I could just go off and work my butt off for four hours, so I was just physically dead tired and then I would go to sleep, just absolutely wear yourself out.

That difference, too, can be a problem if one partner does not understand how normal such a difference is and how important activity (or inactivity) is to the other partner.

Wanting to Have Another Child

In some couples one parent (usually the woman) becomes more invested than the other in having another child. This difference too can be a source of difficulty in the couple relationship. (For more on this, see chapters 6 and 14.)

Religious Differences

Religious differences can become an issue when a couple has to decide what to do religiously about a critically ill child or what to do about a funeral. But the most difficult religious differences seem to be those that emerge in the months and years after the death in relating to God, the clergy, or organized religion.

Lisa: He took more towards God's thing, and I was mad at God. I have a *right.* That's all I kept sayin'. I have a right to be mad at *any*body. He still, I think, thinks that if he didn't have God he would've committed suicide. But I told him, "Give your*self* some credit. Don't give the credit to God (crying). Give yourself the credit, because *you*'re the one that's doin' it." He'd just tell me that I was wrong, and so most of our fighting the past six years was "God." 'Cause he just kinda took that way, and I took talking to people. He doesn't think there's anything else. That the only (*Nick:* That's so) reason's he's here is for God. God doesn't have to be a part of your life every minute of every day. That's how my feelings are. His are completely different. He grieved in that way, and I was grieving in a different way.

In some couples there are differences in religious understanding of the death.

> *Gail:* It's changed the way that I think about God. And for a while it was very uncomfortable to be in church, and I found myself going only to see the other people, and for the friendship and support that I got from these people, and not because of my religious beliefs. And I used to believe that God was all controlling of everything, and that He was the one that made every circumstance be the way that it was. I no longer believe that. I believe that He has the power to control things, but He chooses not to. So *my* point of view has changed, but not my basic belief in Him.
>
> *Vince:* It's funny how we have different justifications (*Gail:* We do). Yeah. I still believe God has control over everything, and I still believe to this day that He took Randy away from us. But I know that when I get to heaven that He's gonna give me the right answer.

Differences in religious understandings can be particularly hard in some couples because religion is for one or both partners a primary path to finding meaning in the death and meaning in life. If partners differ religiously, compromising can be very difficult because to do so can feel like choosing to make the death or life meaningless. If your differences are that significant, it seems to me that the best strategy is to figure out how to tolerate and even support those differences.

Differences Because Partners Grew Up in Different Families

A couple has to come to terms with thousands of differences they bring from growing up in different families, including how to deal with death and how to grieve. It is not necessarily easy to come to terms with such differences when one is grieving. Many spouses may take differences as a reflection of the partner's personality, but the differences are also matters of doing what one was brought up to do, loyalty to parents and grandparents, doing what seems to be right, and being a good person.

Some partners choose not to follow the patterns and standards of their parents and grandparents on matters related to their child's death. That could make it easier to go along with the spouse, though it costs one harmony with parents, siblings, grandparents, aunts, and uncles. But some partners still try to please their parents and grandparents, which can be a source of conflict or discomfort in the couple relationship.

Cultural Differences

Lots of couples come from different ethnic or cultural backgrounds. A couple may think they have reached the point where their ethnic or cultural differences are minimal, perhaps more matters of food preference than anything else, only to discover that a child's death brings out strong cultural differences. Examples might include how or how much to grieve, how to understand the death, or what etiquette to expect from people paying their condolences. I think it is a rare couple with different cultural backgrounds who will not differ in how they grieve in ways that are consistent with those differences.

Expect and Tolerate Difference

The main point of this chapter has been that you should expect and tolerate differences between you and your partner. Doing so is not likely to make the grieving process any easier, but it should help you and your spouse to maintain a stronger couple relationship as you deal with the death of your child.

5

Grief Can Make Marital Trouble

Rosa: I can remember saying to my husband a couple of months after Wendy died that I felt like we were two survivors of a shipwreck and were floating in an ocean, neither of us being strong enough to pull the other one up to save them.

Grief drains parental energy, makes it hard to talk or listen, and blocks or weakens many of the other things that couples ordinarily do that make their marriage work. The marital relationship is not what it was before the child died. At the same time, however, the death creates intense new needs. The combination of neediness and being unable to provide the same support as before is normal, but it leads to what some parents feel is marital trouble. In this chapter I explain why such trouble happens and ways couples can deal with and get past these problems.

Greater Neediness and Less Ability to Meet Needs

Grieving partners may demand more from each other than they can provide—more care, more attention, and more help. At the same time, it is hard to be there for one another.

> *Glenda:* When you both share the same pain, it's hard to help each other with it. And we *did* talk about that. Or I talked, and forced my husband to listen.

Some spouses feel so disgusted with their partner's apparent lack of support they wonder whether the marriage should continue.

> *Rosa:* In the beginning we were fairly close. It's sort of afterwards that *you* got depressed, and quiet. I got gottagettagottagettagotta with my sister and my mother and best friend. I know my mum kept saying, "I don't like how Henry looks." She kept trying to hug you, and you (laughing) wouldn't even let her. There was times when things were really shaky for us as a couple, I think, just because Henry was so quiet.

It may help to speak up about what you need. It also may help to be patient with your spouse and the long, slow process of grieving. Perhaps the most important realization, however, is that even in the best of times, a spouse rarely can meet all one's needs for conversation, understanding, and emotional support. Friends, relatives, colleagues, members of the clergy, counselors, people in support groups—there are lots of people out there who may be able to help.

The Energy Shortage of Grief

In their grief, bereaved parents often have little energy to talk, listen, or do things with their partner. They feel tired and fatigued. You may be worried or upset with this lower level of talking, listening, and doing things. You may feel frustrated or worried at getting less from your partner or giving less to your partner. But if you understand that this is a normal response and trust that energy eventually will return, you can minimize worry and upsetness.

Less Patience, More Nastiness, and Anger

Grieving can make a person less patient, more nasty, and more quick to flame up in anger. It is common for grieving parents to act this way, but it is hard for the partner who becomes a target–especially when these things flare up more frequently than in the past and often arise over the littlest things.

> *Joy:* I do remember one time we were at the store, and I wanted to buy a pen, and you just like had an utter fit. We were going to visit another couple that night. Oh, gol, we didn't even go to their house, and they wondered where we were, and it was over a pen. We have lost a daughter, and we are arguing about a pen. I was going to buy this pen, and you were just like, "You do not need another pen!"

Sometimes a partner realizes that the newest spat is not about what it seems, but actually about the child dying.

> *Gail:* I do remember one of us getting mad at the other. I can't remember which one it was, but one of us was saying to the other, "Are you mad at me, or are you mad because Randy died?" I don't remember what that was over. The other one said, "Oh, I'm not mad at you; I'm mad because Randy died. I'm screaming at you or throwing things at you because Randy died, not because you did anything. You're just there." And I can't even remember which way that went.

When either of you is irritable, you each might back away from talking or even being around one another. Sometimes it can help to keep your distance for a few hours or even a day or two, giving your irritability or your partner's a chance to weaken or go away. Sometimes it helps to have the conversation that Gail discussed, asking whether you or the partner are mad at the other partner or mad because the child has died.

Conflict Over How Open to Be with Each Other

Some couples argue about how open to be with each other in their grief. Conflict is often a good thing, serving as a necessary part of solving problems and maintaining or restoring intimacy. It can make the marriage a good place for both partners. But that does not mean that you will enjoy grief-related conflict or that it will necessarily be constructive. Sometimes it is the wrong time to try to make a change, and some things cannot be changed, at least not now or not the way you are trying to change them. A common conflict in couples is over her way of grieving versus his, with the difference often that one wants more privacy in grieving and the other more sharing.

> *Angela:* Jack grieves by himself, and I know that. And it's like I used to bang my head against the wall.
> *Jack:* At the top of our lungs and the heat of anger? We've (laughing) discussed it that way. When I finally (*Angela:* Tell me to leave you alone) get to the point where I say, "Get off my back," it comes out in that kind of a discussion. But, yeah, to a certain degree I want to be left alone. I know internally how I work. I know what is going to get me through the day. And I would appreciate it that people would let me get through the *day.*

Angela: "You are just to leave me alone." That's kind of how you say it, too (speaking slowly and distinctly): "Leave me alone."

Jack: It just means don't nag me, don't *press* for things that aren't coming.

Angela: And I do. I push him, 'cause I want him to be able to open up to me. If you can open to anybody it should be your wife. But he can't open up. I never win. But I do push, and I don't quit either. Then, of course, that just pisses him off (laughing). But I *try* real hard. I don't ever get what I want, 'cause he's stubborn.

Sometimes the issue is what to make of the other's behavior. My advice is not to take a spouse's quietness or distance personally or to take a spouse's pushing you to be more open personally. Be tolerant of each other's ways of grieving. You also might try to take turns giving the other what the other wants. But I also am not opposed to conflict and argument. It is one way to be with each other, to learn more about one another, and to solve problems.

Blaming

Many bereaved parents think again and again about what happened to the child and about how things could have been different. In the process they often blame themselves or their partner for the death. Blaming is so common that I can say it is normal, but it also can be painful and drive a wedge between spouses.

Lisa: He tol' me he blamed me.

Nick: For a lot of years, that's the number one thing. It wasn't really true, but I was just looking for ways to fight her, I think. I don't know why. "She didn't give him

all the attention what he needed at that time. Why did-
n't she hear him right away?" That's the main thing I
thought all the time.

Paul: When you thought he was blaming you, what
did you do?

Lisa: I just said, "Think what you want to think."
They even told us right at the hospital, he would've had
to been on a operating table, and cut open, for him to
live. Aneurysm is something that just happens that fast,
and there's nothing anybody can do.

When it is the partner who is blamed, the relationship
can be very uncomfortable and can even seem unlikely to
continue. In my experience, however, couples typically manage to leave the blaming behind, and with it the discomfort
and the hard, hard feelings.

How do couples do this? I think a key reason blaming
eventually is left behind is people come to accept that what
has happened has happened, regardless of what they think
or say. Couples come to realize that blaming the spouse won't
help; it only drives a wedge into the middle of the marital
relationship.

Another way some people back away from blaming the
spouse is by deciding that what happened was God's will,
that it was God, not a human being, that made things happen the way they did.

I think many people who blame a spouse realize, as did
Nick, that doing so is not rational or fair and that it is pushing the partner away. And many people on the receiving end
of what they consider undeserved blame help to end the
blaming, as did Lisa, by not buying into it.

Sometimes a spouse directly causes a death. For some
couples to whom that occurs, such as when a parent acci-

dentally backs a car over a child, there is no blaming. But in others, blaming can be harsh. One way a spouse can get past blaming the other in such situations is to recognize that what happened was an accident, not a choice. Accidents happen to everyone; all human beings make mistakes.

Alcohol and Drugs

As I discuss more fully in chapter 11, grief can lead to the abuse of alcohol or drugs, sometimes leading to serious marital problems. Then the path to a good relationship may have to pass through a chemical dependency treatment program, whether it is Alcoholics Anonymous, a clinic-based program, a therapy program, or something else.

Struggles Over Time Together or Apart

All couples get along with a balance of physical and emotional togetherness and apartness. Too much or too little of either may make at least one partner uncomfortable. Too much togetherness can be smothering. Too little can feel neglectful or not attached enough to keep the marriage going. Achieving a balance is difficult because people need different amounts of closeness or distance at different times. Many couples, even in the best of times, have disagreements, power battles, or hard feelings over this issue—troubles that can be intensified by a child's death.

One partner may need more togetherness or more distance than in the past, more than the spouse is comfortable with. Sometimes patterns present before the death become more pronounced. In grief, someone who previously wanted more time alone than the other wanted (or was comfortable providing) may want even more solitude. Conversely, someone who ordinarily wanted more contact than the other desired (or was comfortable having) may seek to be together even more. Also, each of you can fear being dragged into deep sadness by being around the other when the other is down. That might make one of you try to stay away from the other.

Sometimes when the partner who wants more contact tries to make that happen, the other partner is driven even further away. Sometimes one partner moves out of the house temporarily, to get enough distance. Sometimes one partner needs the other to be out of the house now and then, perhaps for just a few hours, to have the freedom to scream, weep, or be alone with private thoughts.

If a difference exists in how much time together or apart the two of you want, my advice is to accept it and see if you can work out ways to be together some of the time and apart some of the time. That way both of you can get some of what you want.

Communication Walls

Grieving can seem to build a communication wall between spouses.

> *Paula:* (very loud) There's times I feel like there's a wall between us since then, maybe partly because we have not sat down and really talked about it and let our feelings out on the accident, because we really have not, the two of us. So to me it has put up a wall between us, but not to the point where we'd leave each other. It's just there.

I think such walls are common, and they can go up for many reasons. For example, one or both of you may not want to face the pain of a conversation about the death, may fear blaming or other harsh words, may not want to talk until things are thought through better, or may just not feel ready to talk. Typically communication walls are temporary, but they can seem insurmountable while they are up. In some couples, the partners manage, over the long run, to communicate by doing it little by little, sometimes without even saying things directly. For example, Paula and her husband, when they finally talked, knew a lot about what each felt and seemed to be in almost complete agreement about everything. If the wall seems more solid, if communicating little by little or indirectly doesn't seem to work, my advice is to be open about wanting to talk and to be patient. (For more advice, see chapter 8.)

Unpleasant Things May Come to the Surface

Following the death, unpleasant things may surface about the partner or marriage that never have done so before although they always were present. It can be hard to deal with those or any problems while grieving, but the fact they have emerged means they must be acknowledged and first steps taken to deal with them. Perhaps the best first step to dealing with any problem is talking respectfully about it and listening respectfully to what your partner has to say. You don't have to agree, but if you can understand each other that is often a good start.

Grief Can Magnify the Problems a Couple Had Before the Death

For some couples who had previous marital problems, grief can magnify their difficulties. Problems that were hard to deal with before the death can become intolerable afterward.

One woman talked about how she could no longer tolerate living in her husband's shadow following the death of their son. Another woman talked about how their poor marital communication became more of a problem following the death of their two children. Thus, for some couples, the major problem to be solved, alone or with professional help, is not their grief but a previous problem that has been magnified by the death.

Conclusion

Grief does not remain the same, and neither do marital problems connected to the grief. Patience with the process may be enough, as things will change, but there also are things you can do. One strategy that sometimes works is to find the good in what is giving you difficulty. For example, if you are annoyed that your spouse is so quiet and distant, think about how this means your spouse cares about the child who died and is grieving in order to come to terms with the loss. Or if your spouse is grumpy, realize how much pain your spouse must be feeling because of the death.

It also is helpful to realize that people often lack the resources to be there for each other when both are grieving. That means each of you may have to go outside the relationship at times to find the listening and support you need. Just as you would not expect to be capable of serving as full-time nurses to the other after both of you had undergone major surgery, neither can youu expect to meet all of each other's needs when you are both grieving.

Instead, be patient. Many problems eventually will become less serious or disappear entirely. But if intolerable problems exist, do something about them. For example, if you are living with physical abuse or the threat of it, a pattern of hurtful communication, or irresponsible use of alcohol, recognize that it is a problem and get help. You may be able to do something about those problems on your own, but professional help may be very important, especially when physical safety is at risk.

Things may not be easy, but that does not mean they are hopeless. Even in the face of enormous problems, many bereaved couples come through to the other side, achieving a deeper, closer, and stronger relationship.

6

"The Sexual Part of Our Relationship Died"

AFTER A CHILD'S DEATH, many couples experience a break in their sexual relationship–one that can last for weeks, months, or even years. Lots of things work together to make it happen, including lower energy levels, stress, a desire to avoid pleasure, emotional distance from a spouse, feeling too depressed, or a wish to avoid something that could set off intense feelings of grief. In describing how she backed away from sexual intercourse, Amy talked about feeling too fragile emotionally.

Amy: I was too fragile. It's sorta like real thin tissue paper; you feel like you could break absolutely any moment.

The Meanings of Sexual Intercourse

Everything that blocks sexual intercourse and everything that makes a couple get back together sexually is related to the meanings sexual intercourse has for a couple. What can block sexual intercourse after a child dies–or make it intense and different from the past when you start again–is what it

72

means to the two of you. There are six meanings that often arise in the sexual relationship of grieving parents.

Intercourse Is How We Made the Child

Some parents who are grieving the death of a birth child think about how sexual intercourse created the child. That can make intercourse less desirable or more emotional.

> *Glenda:* For a long time it was like that's how we got him. Get away! I couldn't. Remember how I cried? (*Ken:* Ooh, yeah.) I think more for me it was very painful emotionally, for a while though (*Ken:* Yeah). And I don't do that anymore, but it was like, we *created* him this way. We can't do this.
>
> * * * * *
>
> *Erika:* I do specifically remember the first time we made love after David died that we both cried. And I think for me it was, "That's how we started his life." And it was just hard.

If Sex Means Pleasure, Now Is Not the Time

For some couples, a break in sexual contact occurs because for one or both partners the pleasure from sex does not fit with their feelings of grief or with the sense of what should go on in grief.

> *Paula:* For a long time after I didn't want to have anything that would bring any type of pleasure, and you just kind of go through the motions of life, and that's it. And that just wasn't a part of it. You could barely get through the day just normal functioning, getting yourself up out of bed, getting yourself to work, giving the basic needs for your kids. That was about all anybody could handle, certainly all I could handle.

In a couple who eventually divorced, there were serious problems because the woman thought that the man wanted to have sexual intercourse the night after their two daughters died. His sexual interest had meanings that did not fit with her grieving and seemed to her to be insensitive to her feelings.

> **Molly:** I found it disgusting. I thought, "The kids are dead and this is all you can think about." That really bothered me. From then on I probably made my mind up to go it alone.

We Can't Do This If It Means Making Another Child

For some parents, the fear of pregnancy is connected to the break in sexual relationship. If either partner feels unprepared to face another pregnancy or parenting another child, even with birth control that seems 100 percent reliable, there can be feelings of not wanting to take the risk.

She: We Should Do This to Make Another Child

Some couples resume sexual intercourse with the woman making it clear that the primary goal is conceiving another child rather than pleasure. That can energize their sexual relationship, but it also can change things for the man in ways that make him uncomfortable.

> **Scott:** Normally, our sexuality, I've always been the aggressor and my desire level is, let's say there's a significant gap between mine and hers. After Gina's death and once we were able to conceive, it was like the shoe was on the other foot. So I did avoid it. The shoe was *really* on the other foot. Not to say that Tina always avoids it, but that's kind of the situation. I did feel pressured, and because of that pressure I was indifferent, and in some cases would try to avoid the situation.

Tina: There was a lot of tension about that, a lot of fights. If he thought that we were gonna be close to being sexual, he'd do everything in his power not to do anything. And I can remember this one night just sitting up here just sobbing and being so sad because we had *both* agreed we were gonna have another child. But then I didn't think he was playin' his part in it. And I remember, goin' through my mind, "That's it! We're done! I'm divorced! I'm leavin' him!"

Now We Are Back Together and Living Life

A return to sexual intercourse together can be a symbol that life is once again worth living, a life that includes marital love and sexual pleasure. Because of its links to love and because sex gives meaning to love and draws meaning from it, sex can be a bond that helps to hold a couple together and to renew the couple relationship.

Paul: Do you remember when you first got together sexually after the death?

Scott: Gee, it was, what's the name of the hotel?

Tina: (laughing) Got the "bridal suite," (*Scott:* yeah), gave them my sob story, even got a *dis*count on the room (laughs), because, "Oh, we had this baby that died, and now we're going off just by ourselves." "Oh, Jeez. We'll give you some off" (laughs). We just went for one night. We had a Jacuzzi, so it was (chuckle) X-rated.

Paul: How long after the death?

Tina: (laughing) Probably six weeks to the day. I surprised him. I had him meet me, and we were gonna have dinner, and then I pulled out this key to the hotel room. "We're gonna go stay in this hotel over night." "O-oh!" We had fun. It was nice to just get away, and kinda get back in touch with each other. We had a really good time. That was when we were feeling at our closest.

He: Intercourse Comforts Me

Some men want sexual contact partly because it means comfort to them, a way to ease pain of any sort, including the pain of a child's death. (Perhaps some women also feel that way, but I have not heard any bereaved mother talk about intercourse in that way.) When the woman does not feel that intercourse is comforting, the couple can find that their different meanings can lead to difficulties.

> *Gail:* As far as (laughter) having sex, I can remember wanting to throw up, because I thought it was just horrible and how could you possibly think of that. I do remember you saying that that made you feel close, and that was comforting for you. But I know that we felt opposite that way.

Touching in Grief

I think of touching as part of sexuality and so do lots of grieving parents. From that perspective, even if you experience a break in sexual intercourse, you may not experience a break in the "touching" part of sexuality. You might actually find yourselves hugging, holding, and touching more than before the death. The touching may be comforting in itself and it may be loaded with positive meanings, such as connection, support, understanding, caring, and comfort.

Sometimes one partner cannot give the physical contact the other wants. Typically, those who hold back interpret the demand for more contact as meaning that their grieving is not being respected or that they are being asked to provide beyond their ability or comfort to do so. Conversely, those who want more contact interpret the low level as meaning that they are not being given needed connection, support, and comfort. It is easy to see how couples with differing feelings and understandings in this area could get into difficulty.

> *Brett:* There was a lot of things I needed, but I didn't get from her. Just even the hugging, the holding, even some talking about it. And it wasn't her job to fix me. There wasn't anybody that was capable of doing that.
>
> *Joan:* I think there would've been times even when he *wanted* to hug me or he wanted to give me support, and I just didn't want it. I just felt like I wanted to deal with my grief myself.
>
> *Brett:* That was uncharacteristic, that you weren't there.
>
> *Joan:* I didn't know I wasn't there for you.
>
> *Brett:* I was up in a lot of nights. I'd be crying in the middle of the night, and you'd just be sleeping.

Early in grief, Iris needed physical contact and Todd could not provide it. Later, he wanted to start having sexual intercourse again, but she was not ready.

> *Iris:* I felt very alone. He's strong and he's steady, but he's not emotional; he's not a hugger. And I felt like I needed a hug now and then or some more physical comfort.
>
> *Todd:* Yeah, I'm not a hugger.
>
> *Iris:* No. You never have been. That wasn't anything new. But I'd lay in bed and cry at night, and he'd lay over near me and be embarrassed and not know what to do. I just felt lonely. And I guess sometimes I resented that.

Todd: Yeah, I didn't know exactly how to handle it when she'd be crying. Didn't know what I could do to make her feel better. Also, I was more interested in intercourse than she was. And so that was kind of a source of frustration to me. I was looking for things to be more like they had been before Jeff was in the hospital, and that simply didn't happen after he died. It was a long time before things changed. Just felt like to me it was an emotional issue. And that would help me feel better. And it helped her feel better not to (both laugh) have any, so I had (both still laughing) a little problem there.

Iris: I just wasn't interested. I don't know why (laughs). My interest was a very gradual thing returning.

Affairs

Some grieving parents have sexual affairs following their child's death. While the affair might have nothing to do with the child's death and the couple grieving, sometimes it seems to. For Steph, the affair meant she was wanted by somebody and she could escape the meanings that sexual contact with her husband had–meanings related to his grief, neediness, and emotional unavailability. Molly, even though she resented her husband's affairs, said she could understand how they were connected to his need to heal.

An affair is not necessarily a long-term problem in a couple's relationship and does not necessarily undermine the relationship. George could forgive and could understand Steph's affair in the context of the loss.

George: I didn't feel threatened by it. What I found particularly sad, because it dawned on me that for her to do that, that she must really be hurting. I didn't want to get even or beat somebody up or go do something stupid myself. It was just very sad.

Returning and Not Returning to Sexual Intercourse

Some couples, even several years after a child's death, have not returned to an active sexual relationship. In some couples with such a break, partners speak of learning to be patient.

> *Bruce:* You don't put a time frame around grieving. You can't say grief will last a month, a year, two years. You can't put a time frame around it. You learn to be patient. If your sex life is bad for a year or two or more, you just go on. So we've been very patient with each other.

For some couples who resume having intercourse, the return is unremarkable. For others, intercourse after the child dies is—at least at first—especially intense, emotional, and connecting, partly because of the emotional sharing they have gone through in dealing with the death.

For some couples who resume sexual intercourse in order to make a child, intercourse may become unpleasantly mechanical. Also, in some couples, just when it looks like the break in sexual intercourse is ending, it takes on a new life if the woman wants to become pregnant and the man does not want to make a baby or does not want that to be the focus of a sexual encounter.

> *Rosa:* Right after she died it was sort of, "I want a baby, so let's have sex." It basically killed our sex. That part of our relationship died, and it's *still* not back to where I'd like it to be. It was really hard to get Henry

excited (laughs) about anything for a long time. And if I pushed or tried to seduce, it made you run away. That part of our relationship is not back to where I'd like it to be. I think that's the biggest change in our relationship since having Wendy die.

Grief during Sexual Intercourse

In some couples, strong feelings connected to the death may come up while making love. For them, intercourse is particularly emotional or intense because of the meanings of intercourse and of the death.

> *Joy:* I remember always just really crying after we had sex, just sobbing and sobbing, and just bringing so many emotions to the surface, and I used to think "Aw, he's going to quit making love to me 'cause all I do is sob afterwards."

> * * * * *

> *Jane:* One thing I've noticed, any time we were intimate, almost always, even though I wasn't sobbing or anything like this, just the emotion. Almost every time one or the other of us would say, and it just really didn't exactly relate, and yet we just really missed Adam. You just were emotional, and that was the biggest emotion in our lives. We just missed Adam, and so frequently I would get tears in my eyes, or Rob would, and we would just say to each other, "I sure still miss him."

Grief during or immediately after intercourse might worry a partner, but my suggestion is to see it as a normal experience and a sign of how a child's death can affect every part of your life. In fact, the grief can be a sign that your sexuality has achieved a down-to-the-core emotional connection between the two that can only be found in the strongest of marital relationships.

Conclusion

Having a child die changes everything, so it should be no surprise if it affects your marital sexuality. If grief dominates your life, it obviously will affect your sexual relationship. My advice is to accept the changes and the differences between the two of you. To deal with whatever is going on (or not going on) sexually between the two of you, work hard at understanding your own feelings and the meanings you give to sexuality, to communicate those understandings to your partner, and to understand–to truly understand–your partner's feelings and meanings.

7

Money

MONEY CAN SEEM of no importance when compared to a child's death, the intense long-term feelings of parental bereavement, and the serious marital difficulties a bereaved couple may face. But money is often part of the struggle for couples, and financial problems connected to the death may place a great deal of additional stress on the relationship. Although some bereaved couples do not have money problems, others have very serious ones. So in addition to all of the other terrible things that happen when a child dies, a couple can find themselves facing tremendous economic obstacles as well.

Bills and Making Do with Less

For some couples, the financial costs of a child's terminal illness and death are very heavy. You may not have had insurance coverage for your child's illness. Or if you did, the insurance may have covered only part of the expenses because of co-pay requirements, because certain medications or treatments were not covered, or because you exceeded the insurance reimbursement limit. Perhaps, too, you ran into one of the many strange ways that insurers and HMOs refuse to pay for what seems appropriate and necessary.

To compound the financial difficulties, some couples are billed for medical services and treatments the child never received or charged more than once for the same services and treatments. You may have the burden of figuring out which bills are fair and which are in error, then trying to straighten out the errors.

Kathy: We had a lot of bills (small laugh).

Karl: Yeah, it was hard. I remember it being very, very hard.

Kathy: Yeah, it was Blue Cross Blue Shield fee for service, so there was a lot of out-of-pocket expenses, and all the doctors we saw. I remember making out the bills and crying all the time, 'cause I had to decide which ones to pay.

Karl: Because we didn't have enough money coming in to pay them all.

Kathy: Yeah, it was always an extra $400, $500 a month or something, and this was a long time ago, too. But we paid them ourselves.

Karl: We don't like owing people, and that was real hard for us. We just didn't have it, and knowing that we were gonna pay, we just didn't know how long it would take. And I remember, we even got calls from some. One of the bills was like a duplicate, too.

Kathy: I had to go through all of the bills (*Karl:* Ah, jeez). There were *so* many errors on them, and we got bills for appointments after the children had died. (*Karl:* Yeah.) There are some real horror stories. They charged for two incubators, and the lady would say, "Are you sure you didn't have twins?" That's a stupid question.

Karl: We got bills for her discharge but she had died, and even for an X-ray after she was buried.

Kathy: I said to them, "So why don't you get a copy of it and tell me what the results were?" They never called me back.

Funerals, too, can put parents thousands of dollars into debt with the cost of caskets, burial plots, and other heavy expenses.

While trying to pay off medical and funeral bills, you may be forced to put the rest of your economic lives on hold. You might not buy new clothes. You may eat only low-cost food and mostly at home. You may make do with a car in bad shape or with no car at all. You may entertain little or not at all. In short, you might be forced to cut every conceivable economic corner. For some couples, doing so may not be difficult. For others, however, there are serious quality of life issues that hurt the couple relationship. For some couples, living without a car or with an old one, eating only cheap meals, forgoing visits to out-of-town relatives, sending surviving children to school in ill-fitting, old clothes, and having almost no money for gifts can rock the marital relationship.

Quitting a Job in Order to Deal with a Child's Illness

To compound the financial difficulties, one parent often has to quit earning an income when a child becomes very sick. That parent devotes full-time to caring for the child, visiting the hospital, and managing the complexities of dealing with insurers, doctors, the politics of managed care, and the confusion around diagnosis and treatment. The loss of that parent's income usually leads to greater financial difficulty, which in turn can set off problems within the household and with the larger family.

Grief that Undermines Money-Earning

For some parents, grief undermines their ability to earn money. Even if you do not lose a job or a business, your income may suffer. You may be slow to finish income-generating work. You may make costly mistakes. You may find yourself unable to do some of the necessary parts of the job. You may be distracted or neglectful in ways that cut down your income—for example, by making difficulty with customers or employers.

In one couple, the man's loss of concentration because of his grief and his concerns about his wife's deep depression led the couple to worry about his losing his job.

> *Louise:* When it was affecting his job, I was real concerned. I thought, "What on earth would we do if he lost his job?" And the concentration factor. He would have to go to people's houses and measure, more concentration type things. I know he was real concerned about what if he lost his job. Then what are we gonna do? That was the only reason I even agreed to go into counseling. I was basically told either you do or he's gonna, 'cause he needs counseling, and the counselor felt it had to be a joint effort. Just having him go into counseling wasn't gonna help. Unless we both went, it wasn't gonna work, and if I wasn't agreeable to go, then it was gonna continue to affect his job, and ultimately he would lose his job.

If grief does lead to the loss of a job, the family's ensuing economic problems can create marital as well as financial difficulties.

> *Brett:* I lost my job 'cause I was supposed to be sellin', but I was depressed, and I couldn't sell anything.

Joan: I wasn't happy about it.

Brett: And I wanted her to say, "It's okay" (chuckling).

Joan: I didn't blame him for it. I just thought, (exasperated sigh) "What next? Now what? Now what are we gonna do?" But it probably came off that I was blaming him, but I didn't mean it that way, but I didn't know (exasperated, whining:) "Where do we go from here?"

Even if a new job is found, it may not pay what the previous job did, and the lost income may never be replaced.

Dealing with Your Financial Problems

The path of a marriage is easier when there is enough money for necessities and at least some luxuries. When money is tight, couples are more likely to get into power battles and painful conflicts over what to do with the money they have. They may give up things that help their marriage to work better–restaurant meals, vacations, movies.

Money problems may be compounded by how those problems affect a couple's relationships with the larger kin group. If, for example, they cannot afford to visit distant relatives, give appropriate gifts, or offer appropriate financial help, that may lead to rifts within a family. And such problems may increase the couple's marital problems. For example, if you are not able to contribute financially to a parental anniversary celebration, the parents and other family members may be upset. And their anger can make things harder for you and your spouse.

Conclusion

What can you do? The most important step is to understand that increased expenses and reduced earnings are likely to put further strains on a marriage and that financial difficulties are common among bereaved couples. Don't take the money problems personally. Don't be hard on yourself or your partner. People do get back on their feet financially. But it may take a while. If your money problems seem serious, get help. A relationship counselor may help with your decision-making as a couple about finances. A financial counselor may help you with money management. A lawyer may help with ways to manage debts. A grief counselor may help with grief that seems to be undermining income-getting ability. An employment counselor, friends with contacts, or a job-seeking support group may help with finding a new job. Be patient with your financial problems, but also know that there is help out there that can make a difference.

8

Talk

Couple Talk Can Help a Lot

I HAVE INTERVIEWED couples who decades after their child's death say they scarcely ever talked about the death or its effect on them. So I know there are couples who stay together without much, if any, talk about the death and what it set in motion in their lives. I also know that there cannot be much talk until both partners are ready. This chapter presents a balanced view of why talking can be good, what to expect from it, and how to get into it, while also dealing with why not talking can be good for some couples and why forcing talk can make trouble.

Talking will almost always give you a better idea of what the other thinks and feels. You will understand yourself better, too, because talking can help you to think more clearly and to figure things out. Almost always it is easier to be supportive if you know more of the other's thoughts and feelings. When you talk little or not at all, you more often will guess wrong about what the other thinks and feels. (You probably also will guess right a lot of the time, but without talk you will miss important things.) Without talk, grieving is lonelier. Without talk, your relationship is in some ways more distant.

I am not saying that there is anything you *should* talk about or that the talk has to be deep or spiritual. Sometimes just a few words about a memory, a feeling, or a dream, sometimes just a brief question makes a big improvement in getting along with each other and in mutual understanding.

If you have not talked much if at all about your child's death, considerable anger may come out the first few times you discuss it. One of you may resent the other's not talking, or perhaps one of you may resent the other's trying to start a conversation about the topic. The first few times you talk after not doing so for a long time it is likely that part of what you discuss will be resentment. That's good. Those feelings and thoughts need to come out. They are the first steps on a path toward a better relationship.

Even if almost everything you have to say is something the other knew or guessed correctly, talking still can be good. Talking can give both of you feelings of getting things out in the open, feelings that were hard to keep bottled up. It can provide relief and a sense that your marriage is getting stronger than it was. Talking can help you to feel closer and more like your partner is really your partner.

I am not saying you must talk, however, and I am not saying that you should talk now. Many grieving couples will avoid discussing the death for long periods, and couples also communicate in important and powerful ways without words. You communicate by touching, paying attention, hugging, sighing, making facial expressions, and acting like you care or do not care about what is going on with your partner. Sometimes it is not so important to one spouse that the other does not talk for a while as it is how the other remains silent and why the other says he or she does not want to talk. Obviously, if you don't care about or respect your spouse, not talking is a symptom of bigger marital problems.

But if you each care about the other and are patient with the things that must happen before you both are ready to talk, you may be doing fine without talking.

Why Not Talking or a Long Delay in Talking Is So Common

Grief is in part private, meaning you will never know completely what your partner deals with, feels, and thinks. Nobody will. Much of your grieving takes place in your minds and when the other is not around.

> *Joan:* If I felt like I needed to cry, it was more like when I was alone. Or if I was feeling bad and I wanted to get through it, instead of just thinking about it, I would grab something that had a particular memory of Alex. I'd grab a baby blanket, or I'd play the tape that we played the night he died. Or go look through his pictures or his cards. I just wanted to do it alone, rather than share it.

Parts of grieving may also go on alone because with shared grief there will be times when neither of you is in a good place to help the other or talk about what you are feeling.

> *Kathy:* We really couldn't help each other that much. We had to really find it within ourselves to help ourselves.
>
> *Karl:* I don't remember anything from that time. I don't remember a thing.
>
> *Kathy:* Whatever we did numbed us, yeah. I don't remember much. We were just like in another dimension, and operating alongside ourselves, and just kind

of going through the motions of being alive (slight laugh). But not really there, 'cause we don't remember that much.

Karl: And I never realized that. We have not talked about this. And this is the first time I've tried to think, "What were we doing (*Kathy:* yeah), during those times?" And I don't remember a thing from then.

You may, like some couples, avoid topics on which you disagree.

Iris: Sometimes I would say something to him, and he would disagree with me. And I would get upset with him. Then I would just drop it.

You also may, like some couples, stay away from topics that one of you does not like to deal with. For some couples, "what ifs" are such a topic. One of you may want to talk about "what ifs" (what if your child had been diagnosed earlier, what if the two of you had not let the child go out that night), and the other does not want to discuss things that cannot be changed.

Bonnie: You keep thinking, "Well, why couldn't Jill have had surgery and come out of it okay?"

John: Well, that's one of the things that [if] somebody dug into it a little bit more, they probably could've discovered it and taken care of it, but (sniffs) doesn't do any good to dwell on it. It's not going to change things now. (*Bonnie:* No. I don't want to become bitter.) Don't even want to think about that part of it anyway. It doesn't do any good.

Many parents, particularly in the first months after a child's death, seemingly try to avoid talking about things that will bring up strong feelings. They may not want to feel those feelings or cause their spouse to do so. They may want very much to control their own emotions and help their spouse to do the same.

Some couples fear that when they talk they will get into power battles, perhaps particularly about the right way to grieve or what meaning to give to the death. By not talking, they may feel they are at least for now avoiding conflict and that their partner eventually will change so that discussions down the road will not lead to a power battle. Some may fear that talking will cause something bad, perhaps that something will be said that is unforgivable.

Some couples do not talk because they never talk much if at all about heavy matters. If you two did not talk much or easily about heavy matters before, you are not likely to talk much now. Perhaps it is one of the things to get therapy about or join a support group together, to work on talking, if you want to. But perhaps it is just the way your relationship is, and if it is not something either of you aches to change, you will be able to live with it.

Not Talking Does Not Mean
You Are Doomed as a Couple

I want to emphasize again that limited conversation does not mean you are doomed as a couple. Lots will be communicated through other means, and you still will have much in common and know many of the same things. Every couple I have interviewed who said they had not talked or talked only a little about their child's death and its aftermath still had a shared story to tell. They knew and thought many of the same things, had witnessed many of the same things, and agreed on a great deal. They had their differences, but there was still a tremendous amount of agreement.

It also is true that the couples who do talk have their differences and problems. Talking does not necessarily make differences or problems go away. Still, couples generally can reach a better understanding of each other and can agree more on facts and viewpoints with more talk.

Getting to Talk

Many couples who do not talk for a long period ultimately find their way to doing so. It may take a while, and it may be challenging, but they will get there. But if one or both of you are thinking you should reach that point soon, I have some things for you to think about.

Some people are not ready, so forcing talk won't work. But sometimes, even if one partner seems unprepared, even a little bit of talk helps. And sometimes even a small start can open the floodgates, making it easy and valuable to talk a lot.

Talk is often the territory of one partner more than the other, and it is important to remember that the less vocal spouse is dealing with feelings in other ways. Do not equate not talking with not grieving. People who throw themselves into physical activity, reading, work, private quietness, or something else are still dealing with the loss. Speaking as someone who sometimes grieves in solitary ways, I also must say that sooner or later it cannot be all solitary; you have a relationship to care for. Even if talk does not seem necessary to you, it can be very helpful.

To achieve quality talk, it helps to be a good listener–to try to understand your partner's words and meanings and show that you understand. That means being together without distractions. Turn off the TV, the radio, the CD player. Listen not only with your ears, but also with your mind and your heart. Even if you have differences that shock or amaze you, it helps to acknowledge and respect what your partner says. "Respect" means that you do not say or even imply that your partner is crazy, dumb, ignorant, or anything else negative. It means you hear your partner out and do not try to bully him or her into silence or into saying things not true to what your partner feels and believes.

I think respectful two-way communication is based a lot on "I" statements—"I feel . . . ," "I believe . . . ," "I remember . . . ," and so on. If you make what you say as your view rather than the truth and do not label your partner as wrong if he or she differs from you, dealing with your differences respectfully will be easier. It also helps to be open to correction—for example, of things you misunderstood, forgot, did in error, or said in error.

I think one goal always should be to create a safe environment for continued communication. That requires building feelings of trust and safety by understanding each other, tolerating differences, apologizing (to the extent you can) for things you have done or said that may have hurt or offended your partner, forgiving your partner (to the extent you can) for saying and doing things that have hurt or offended you, and being honest. Sometimes, to make communication work, you have to talk about your talk, to discuss in a respectful way what you think is going on in your communication and where you'd like it to go. (Respect does not mean agreement; it just means accepting what your partner says without attacking or feeling defensive.) Also, I think couples generally should achieve a balance in talking and listening, that it cannot be only one partner talking. But plenty of couples get along fine with one talking much more than the other.

It sometimes helps at the beginning of a conversation to identify what you want to talk about and to review at times where you want to go with your talk. If you do not agree on what to discuss, it may be helpful to compromise or agree to take turns. ("This time we will deal with what you want to deal with; next time it will be my turn. Okay?")

What should you talk about? You decide. One common issue for couples is talk about relationship goals, for example, staying together, keeping the child in memory, and being patient with each other's grieving. A lot of couples also at some time talk about making the child real for others and finding ways to honor or celebrate her or his memory.

Don't Overload the Marital Relationship

Bereaved couples need to be patient with the grief process. That includes patience with both your partner and yourself about talking or about discussing certain things. Trying to *force* yourself or your partner to talk generally does not work well. Putting too much pressure on your marital relationship to get to talk too fast or discussing many things at once can cause both of you to feel frustrated and annoyed.

Another part of not overloading your relationship is to accept that one or both of you may talk a lot with others about the child's death and what has happened since then. The marriage does not have to be the only relationship in which the death and your grief is discussed. In fact, many people talk primarily about the death and their grief with someone other than their spouse. I do not even think it is such a great idea to only talk to your spouse about the death and your grief. For all sorts of reasons, it can be an advantage to have others to talk to.

A Lifelong Conversation

Marital conversation about your child's life, dying, death, and the aftermath is not like checking off something on a shopping list. Your feelings and thoughts about all these things are always in process. There always are revisions, additions, and new interpretations. You will learn new things and come to new perspectives, feelings, and thoughts. Even decades after the death, you still will be working toward a better and more up-to-date story. Gabe and Sue, more than thirty years later, drove four hundred miles to deal with "the loose ends" of their daughter's death.

Gabe: We went back to where we were living when she died, trailered back there, 'cause we hadn't picked up the death certificate, things like this. The loose ends weren't closed up from that. So, called the different places. Called the mortician, and she called the doctor, and he had since died but his wife, now that was thirty-four years ago at that time, she remembered that case very clearly. All the records naturally had been destroyed, but we did get the death certificate and things like that. We just kinda wrapped up the loose ends of stuff.

Sue: I wanted to get the information so I could read it, 'cause we had not. I'd learned a lot in those years in between. Isn't that why we, you wouldn't have pursued that if I hadn't. (*Gabe:* That's right. That's what it was. You had learned more about it and you wanted to read what the cause of death was.) Yeah. That's why we went back. And it was *very* helpful. I think that doing that, as painful as that was (sniffling), I think that probably did more for me to put it in the past than anything. There was something there I needed to

Gabe and Sue simultaneously: see it.

Gabe: When she died some of those words we didn't understand. Now there's some meaning to 'em. We know what they mean and like what the reasons were.

Sue: So that's why we went back. Another aspect of that was I was thinking about our kids and how we knew about this stuff, but we had no document. We had nothing, and maybe they would need that death certificate at some point or the cause of death. I was thinking about what was actually in the autopsy. That was part of it. We're getting older, and our kids are having kids and somehow that was important. We both agreed that that would be important for them to have some of that stuff if they needed it.

Again and again, new things will arise that lead you and your spouse to talk about the child, the death, and what has happened as a result. Even if everything seems in place now, new questions and new reminders will come up.

9

Friends, Relatives, and Coworkers

Sorting People and Being Distanced by Them

Sorting People

BEREAVED PARENTS SAY that friends, relatives, and coworkers differ enormously in how helpful and supportive they are. There are people who seem to know just what to do and say and who provide caring, valuable help, and support. There also are people who not only are unhelpful and unsupportive, but who also act like they are uncomfortable with you, say offensive things, or burden you with their own needs. As you figure out who is good to be with and who is not, you probably will go through a process in which you sort people.

> *Ted:* We were very expressive about what was going on and what happened. Some people could handle it and some people couldn't.
>
> *Amy:* We hung on to the ones that let us be more expressive. It sorta was a natural elimination.

* * * * *

Sally: We sorted friends. We made new friends in our support group, and some of my old friends I stopped seeing.

Bruce: We dropped our closest friends. The woman was somebody who Sally grew up with.

Sally: When Mike died, my friend couldn't handle it. She just didn't know what to say and didn't want to hear me talk. So they stopped being our friends.

Sorting is not necessarily an all-or-none thing. Often it is a matter of being careful about what you say to certain people or what you ask of them. Certain difficult people, particularly close relatives and coworkers you have to see a lot while on the job, you are not likely to drop from your life. You may feel hurt or angry if such people say or do something offensive, but you are less likely to end your relationship with them than either to ask them to change how they deal with you or to find ways to get greater distance from them.

Iris: Some of the nurses from the hospital came to the visitation. And they hung around till most of the other people had left. And then they sat down with me and we were talking. And they told some stories about Jeff. I think that's what set your mom off. She was really mad that those nurses had even come and that they had taken up any of my time.

Todd: Mom is a big one on propriety and manners and all that. She comes from upbringing where you didn't make a scene about anything and you always behaved yourself properly.

Iris: She didn't say that I behaved improperly, but I think she was insinuating that I had.

Todd: And she felt it was improper that the nurses took as much of her time as they did, when other people wanted to have a chance to have some.

Iris: That was the biggest one.

Paul: Did you get into conflict with your mother-in-law?

Iris: Yeah, yeah. We had some heated words (clearing her throat). At home. After, we had words. It was bad enough that they asked if they should stay in a motel. I guess he handled it. I just shut myself in my room (slight chuckle). Anyway, that's been a simmering thing. Relationships between us have been tenuous ever since.

As a result of your child's dying, you may have a new sense of what life and death mean, a changed sense of what is important, new kinds of wisdom, and new sensitivities. Those things may move you to ways of thinking that some of your friends, relatives, and coworkers cannot reach, so sorting also happens because you have, in a sense, outgrown some of the people in your life.

Sorting also comes out of not having the energy or patience to take chances on what certain people will think, say, or do. You may distance others you just are not sure about or from whom you fear the worst.

People Who Distance You

After a child dies, some of your friends, relatives, and coworkers will draw away from you. They may attend the funeral, but never want to talk about the death or anything related to it after that. They may not even want to be near you.

Vince: There aren't that many people that you can talk to about something like this. There are *very* few people. I can remember I said after Randy died, it was like you had AIDS or leprosy (laughing).

* * * * *

Ted: People don't want to talk about especially an infant. Some of it is they're afraid to say something that will offend you or they don't know what to say. So they think if they don't say anything that's the best.

Amy: Oh, "As long as you're doing okay."

Ted: Yeah. "Are you doing okay?" That's basically what you get.

* * * * *

Karl: You almost got the impression that people felt that whatever was wrong was catching. It was like nobody wanted to associate with us then.

Kathy: Like there was something really wrong with us, and I think some friends who were having babies at the time were kind of afraid to be near us, or to be near me. That was particularly hurtful.

Karl: There was definitely a feeling that whatever we had, if we touched anybody, they'd get it and they'd have problems.

Kathy: Or be bad luck or whatever.

* * * * *

Louise: I would go for walks, and I'd see somebody coming towards me a couple of blocks away that I'd recognize, and they'd disappear. I knew they didn't live in that cul-de-sac, but they crossed the street and go off some other way. And I'd tell Wayne (chuckling), "I really feel like I have the plague or something," 'cause people just disappear. I go into a store and I'd see somebody, and they'd disappear. I couldn't understand why people were doing this. They were almost afraid of us, 'cause they'd look at us and they'd think, "Something like this can actually happen to a child. I don't want to have anything to do with these people, because it's reminding me of that."

Some parents say that they feel grief over others pulling away from them. They not only are struggling with the death of the child (though that is the hardest struggle), but they also are struggling with the disappointment and feelings of loss they have about people distancing them.

Distance from Others Pushes You and Your Partner Together

Distance from others leaves you and your partner much more with each other than you were before the child died. In fact, the distancing may even leave you with virtually nobody to be with other than your spouse.

Kathy: It was an awful, awful time. The experiences we had with the outside world were *so* negative, and I think that's partly (sniffles) why we just retreated into the safety of our own home and our son. All those little cruelties, they just built up one by one by one. All that hurtful things, and the insensitive things. They just kind of turned us all away. My family at one point was concerned after our son died that we were staying by ourselves for a while (sniffles), and they, what did they want to send to come over or to check on us? And my brother said, "Leave them alone." They thought, "Oh, they're gonna kill each other. They're (laughing) gonna kill themselves." Or something, and my brother said, "Just leave them alone. They just really want to be alone." I think he understood.

Distance from others means that most men and many women say that they go through long periods in which the only person they talk to much about the child is their partner.

Denny: There's nobody else I'd talk to as much about it as Marsha. They say people always listen, but it's also a very taboo subject.
Marsha: It makes people uncomfortable (chuckles) to talk about dead children.
Denny: Yeah. Maybe it's morbid or something. That's why I guess we rely on each other.

So part of what goes on in your marital relationship is a result of the distancing that you do of others and that others do of you. With others not so available, it can put a heavier load on your marital relationship. That may not be a problem, but it can be, because both of you are needy and will, for a long time, not be in a good place to meet one another's needs. At the same time, the enforced closeness can increase your feelings of unity and closeness with each other.

Finding Supportive Others

Despite the sorting and the distancing, many bereaved parents find people beyond their partner who are supportive and helpful. Some of these may be individuals who were important to you long before your child died, but some may have been casual acquaintances or people you met only recently.
Some parents seek out people with similar experiences.

Chad: For three or four years we got involved with other people and other parents around the country who had lost children this way. And it was just amazing. There was four, five in our state from that year.

Erika: There were four other boys. Now we're talking eighteen or younger that died within six months of David.

Often bereaved parents find helpful others as an individual rather than as a couple. For example, you may turn to a sister or a close friend, and your spouse may turn to a sympathetic cousin or a coworker.

Brett: I have one friend that, he couldn't say anything. He just is not an emotional guy. He doesn't know what to say. But every day he (*Joan:* He feels for you, but he doesn't know how to express it) (laughs) but every single day he would call me up and say, "Hi, how are you doing?" And then I would say, "I'm doing," you know, I would tell him, but it would be blank on the other end (laughs). And I'd have to carry the conversation, but it felt good to know that I had somebody, even though he didn't know what to say.

* * * * *

Kathy: About five years ago, one of my closest friends at work, she had a perfectly healthy baby who the day before school started died of SIDS. (small laugh) I just completely fell apart. And yet she sought me out for help. This woman wanted to know everything about my kids, 'cause I didn't know her at the time when all that happened. And I went to some of her meetings at Children's Hospital, talked to her *every* day that whole school year, every morning we just cried. It was somewhat cathartic for me, too, because I understood what she was saying, and she understood that I understood, and that helped her a lot. So that helped me come to terms with a lot of things that were too painful to talk about. She's the kind of person that just had to talk about everything.

When a partner goes outside the marriage for support and help, it not only is good for the partner but it also usually is good for the marriage. It meets needs that cannot be satisfied so easily within the marriage, thus easing pressure on the couple relationship. Going outside may provide useful perspectives and knowledge that can be brought back into the marital relationship, and it may provide an outlet for frustrations with the partner.

I think it is good to find couple or individual relationships that are supportive. Get your support where you can. But I think it also is important to work at maintaining the marital relationship. If one of you goes outside the marriage for a great deal of support, be sure to keep in contact with your spouse. Check in with your spouse, and be sure that the two of you are communicating well enough about enough to maintain a solid base for knowing each other. That does not mean you have to agree on everything, talk about everything, or even discuss very much, but do not allow yourselves to become strangers.

10

Support Groups and Counseling

HELP COMES IN MANY FORMS, including sympathy cards, community fund-raising dinners, special phone calls, or money donated by friends and church members. Some parents talk about relatives, friends, coworkers, or acquaintances who listen or provide advice. But quite a few say the help available from people they knew was not enough. They had to seek out new sources of assistance, such as a counselor (for example, a grief counselor, pastoral counselor, or marital therapist) or a support group.

Al: We've told a lot of people, if anybody goes through anything like this, I'd say go to a counselor like we did.

Barb: Definitely.

Al: Absolutely the best thing I would advise anybody to do is go see a counselor.

Barb: Yeah, and to get out. Don't just set here and hibernate and vegetate.

* * * * *

Joan: The Pregnancy and Infant Loss Center was a big deal, gave us a lot of information.

Brett: We went to the grief group through the hospital, and it was great. And after that we helped with a lot of, they have like a Christmastime memorial service, and we helped with that a couple of years. And we were on a committee to help other people that were going through the grief group.

Why Do People Go?

You may have friends or family members who can provide the kind of listening, understanding, and wisdom also available from first-rate counseling or a support group, but lots of people go to counseling or a support group for things they cannot get from family or friends. People seek out counseling or a support group because somebody (self, spouse, or someone else in the family) is feeling more grief, pain, fear, emptiness, anger, or anxiety than can be tolerated. Or they go because there are serious difficulties in marital or family relationships.

Denny: I had a tough night, and I called the hot line that's through work, just to talk to somebody, and they gave me referrals to people out in the suburbs, where I won't have to drive twenty-five miles to the hospital where both my children died.

* * * * *

Paul: What led you to try the counselor?

George: Oh, just open the lines of communication. At that point I knew Steph was drinking quite heavily, and that alarmed me, and she had things about me she wanted to get off her chest.

* * * * *

Al: For a long time Barb *would* get mad about different things that I do. That's what you've got to go to a counselor for; you gotta work it out. The older people dealt with it in a different way. A neighbor over here lost a son and a husband, and I went to see her, and she said, "The best thing you can do, go see some counselor. If you don't like the guy, tell him where to go; go see another one. Because there's some good counselors out there and I know they're going to help you. Go talk to them. If you can do it, get Barb to go. If you want me to, I'll talk to her. But go see a counselor. Otherwise you stay mad the rest of your life. I could name you a couple of women that have went through similar things like this. They never get over it. They've lost a child or they lost a husband and they get so bitter. They just plain don't get over it."

Sometimes a part of the push to get help is one of the spouses feeling at wit's end and giving an ultimatum.

Lisa: I always felt like with Nick with God it wasn't helping him for them six years, so it's time to try something else. At one time I told him if he didn't go see a psychologist that that was it. So he went. We got a few things out of that.

One couple went to counseling because the man's employer gave an ultimatum, "Get couple counseling or lose your job."

Wayne: My boss had seen that I was *losing* touch on things, which I could not see myself. This is over a year time span, that first year, and they said that I had to get counseling. So that's when Louise and I had joint counseling. (*Louise:* They forced me into it.) Yeah.

Louise: Wayne didn't really think he wanted to get involved in it, but he does a lot of statistics and num-

bers and they said (*Wayne:* "Stop!") he was making a
lot of mistakes, and so they said, "You need to get into
counseling, and you probably should get your wife,"
and Wayne said, "I don't think she's gonna go." And
they gave you an ultimatum, "Either you both get counseling, or you're going to lose your job."

Some people start counseling or begin attending a support
group because they want to be sure that if something is
wrong, even if they cannot see it, they will get help.

Some people are pressed to go to a support group by the
staff at the hospital where the child died, while some couples start counseling focused on concerns about a surviving
child but then find it useful for themselves as well.

When a couple goes together to counseling or a support
group, often only one of the partners wants to go or feels it
is needed. However, often both eventually benefit and feel
that having gone was the right thing to do.

Sometimes a child's death opens issues not directly related
to the death but that demand professional help. It could be
anything–past or current relationships with your parents,
career and education choices, past losses, self-esteem issues,
you name it.

Sometimes part of the push to attend counseling or a support group is that one partner feels inadequate or unwilling
to provide what the other wants.

Some people say they started out seeking things they
eventually realized no one could provide. For example,
counseling cannot magically make pain go away, nor can it
guarantee that your partner will change. But counseling
and support groups can produce good outcomes, including
benefits you may not anticipate when you first decide to
seek help.

"I Think It Was Healthy for Us"

Counseling and support groups work for all sorts of reasons, and what follows are common things that bereaved parents tell me have been helpful to them.

"An Outlet Other Than Each Other"

In a world where others turn away from bereaved parents and where a spouse can give only so much, support groups or counselors provide someone who can listen to what you have to say about your child's death and the aftermath of the death and who can respond knowledgeably, sensitively, non-judgmentally, and supportively.

> *Ted:* It's like an independent third-party outlook. I think it was healthy for us. It allowed us to have an outlet other than each other and hear some feedback other than just each other. And hear stories other than just ours.

"Somebody to Tell You You're Normal"

Some people want a sense of what is normal and appreciate receiving it.

> *Barb:* You need somebody to kinda put you on the road again. You wonder are you losing your mind, and I think you need somebody to be a stabilizer for you and to tell you if you are or you're not.
> *Al:* To get straightened out.
> *Barb:* Umhm. And I think if you have friends that you can get that from, that's fine. But I think you need professional help, bad. Not meaning that you're losing it, just that you need somebody to tell you that you're not, and that you're normal.

It is hard to feel normal around others who have not experienced the death of a child, so joining a support group is valuable for some parents partly because they feel more normal with others who also have lost a child.

Finding out what is "normal" can be reassuring as you learn that others have had to deal with the same pain and frustration.

Scott: What really helped with the support group is when she expressed those feelings of (*Tina:* Wanting to vomit when you'd see a pregnant lady.) (he chuckles, she laughs), and then feeling guilty 'cause you felt like that. There were other women there that substantiated that feeling. She was thinking, "Gee, I guess I'm not so abnormal after all," 'cause she was thinking, "Am I the only one in the world that feels this way?" They'd start talkin' about, "Yeah! Yeah! That's exactly how I feel!" (she chuckles) It was a boost to understand that, "Gee, these feelings that I have are not that horrible. It's okay. Other people have these feelings."

Tina: Yeah. You're walking around and you're feeling like everybody's devaluing you. And you don't know. "God, am I goin' through this normally? Is this okay?" And going to that support group really validates that you're not weird, 'cause I'm doin' the same kinds of things. I did some really weird stuff.

* * * * *

Rosa: I saw a therapist who specializes in bereavement counseling for people who lost children. I saw him when I was pregnant with our next child and was having real problems with chest pain and depression. It was like six months after Wendy had died, and he was good, 'cause he basically said, "This is gonna hurt.

There's no magic pill. There's nothing I can do. We can sit and talk about this, but you have to work through it, and these are the stages, and, no, you're not dying. You're not going crazy." Basically sort of laid out a road map on "what can I expect?" After Wendy died, remember we said, "Well, I think we feel angry today. This is the anger stage. Okay, we got that (claps hands together) done" (laughing). We read all the books that were out, and we plotted the stages and sort of went, "Okay, now I'm feeling good. Okay, this is depressed, and now I should be done." And then it hits you, 'cause you haven't (chuckling) even really started. That was all just denial at the front. So I found him really quite good.

Finding out what is "normal" can be a good thing, but it can also be distressing if you learn that things could be hard for a long, long time. Nevertheless, it's good to have accurate expectations, and many parents are glad to learn from a support group or counseling that they are like other bereaved parents.

"Telling Our Stories Is Therapeutic"

A support group or counseling professional can help bereaved parents develop their stories that deal with the loss and its aftermath, and in the process help to make sense of things and make life more livable.

> *Vince:* We have been extremely fortunate running across this group called Compassionate Friends. Gail was even a facilitator. So we've had the opportunity to tell our story *hun*dreds of times. And each time you tell it, it's very therapeutic. With something like this it's like you're storage shelf falls out and all these boxes full of

things came unraveled, and each time you talk about it you get a chance to put these pieces back into the boxes and get the shelf organized.

"We Heard What Happened to Other People"

In many support groups, parents differ in the time since their loss. Those differences mean that the parents who have been grieving longer are able to offer hope and knowledge to those parents whose loss is more recent.

> *Vince:* We finally came to the realization that we don't always grieve about the same thing at the same time. We're not always in the same mood. It was nice that we recognized that we grieve at different levels and gave each other the latitude to regress, 'cause you need to regress. You don't go from step one to step two to step three to step four, and never go back to three for a day, and two for a day here, a week, or whatever. You're always going back to step one, two, or three, and you could be going along there for a couple years, and all of a sudden go back to step five (chuckling). That was one of the big things I got out of Compassionate Friends.
>
> *Gail:* We heard that happened to other people, and heard that couples were at different points at different times individually and that was okay. At first we were just very tight and very close, and we just moved re-e-al slow ahead together, and not without each other. We wouldn't move, until whenever the day was that one of us moved a little bit differently. And we started to realize that it was *happening* to us, and it was pointed *out* to us after we went to group and heard it talked about.

Some couples also learn from a support group how to protect themselves from feeling too much pain.

> *Louise:* In the support group they will say how you have to protect yourself. I avoid situations that I know are gonna be depressing.

"We Found New Friends"

Nobody says the main reason they attend a support group is to find new friends, and many people go with little energy for starting new relationships. Yet grieving parents realize they have "lost" many friends and that they need friends with similar experiences of loss able to listen to them talk about their experiences and feelings. Some parents find new friends in a support group and are grateful that has happened.

"It Felt Good to Be Able to Help Others"

Through their work in support groups, some parents become active supporters of other bereaved parents. It is not usually a benefit at first, but, if they stay with a support group, many parents come to feel good about the help and support they are able to provide others.

"You Learn How to Talk"

Some bereaved parents talked about the ways a support group or a counselor helped them communicate as a couple.

> *Al:* You go through something like this, and you've been to counseling and you learn how to talk and not talk and are supposed to have learned how to talk and not swear at one another.

"They Can Relate"

Many bereaved parents feel that they need to be with people who can understand them because of also having experienced a child's death.

Joy: They can relate. It's like no matter how much your friends care and how loving, they can still go home to all their children tucked in bed and they don't know what that feels like. They can't relate to that empty chair and that empty bed. So probably, to be with other couples who have lost a child (*Stan:* yeah), to talk to them. They can really relate to those things.

* * * * *

Wayne: We went to this grief group. It was good for me to get with somebody else that has gone through the same situation. When they said, "We understand how you're feeling, and we know what you're gonna go through," (*Louise:* yeah) they really *mean* that.

Some parents find it especially valuable to be with someone whose loss was similar to their own. For example, one woman whose son died of a rare hereditary disease found another woman who had lost several children to the same disease. To each woman, the other was fascinating and very important.

"A Lot of Wisdom"

Some people talked about wisdom they valued getting from a support group or a therapist.

Joy: We took our son who was hurt in the accident that killed Jenny to a child psychologist. She said one thing, which I thought was really a lot of wisdom, one thing you want to be careful of is thinking that if only Jenny were here life would be perfect. Because, she said, it wouldn't be. And I think that maybe would have been a tendency. I could see where that would be easy to think. Oh, if only Jenny were here things would be perfect or this wouldn't be so bad.

Another woman talked about how a marriage counselor helped her back away from trying to change her husband and believing that he had to change for her to be happy.

Why Counseling or a Support Group Might Be Disappointing

Going Too Soon

Sometimes people are not ready for counseling or a support group. Early in grief you might not have the energy, focus, or pain tolerance to talk about your experiences or to listen to others describe theirs.

Being Unwilling to Do the Work

Some people go to counseling or a support group but are not willing to do the work they are asked to do there. They do not want to answer the counselor's questions, think about certain painful facts, or work at learning what can be learned there.

Partners Who Want Different Kinds of Counseling

Stories about counseling that does not work for couples often can be about personal differences. Not only can couples differ in how they grieve, but they also can differ in the counseling they prefer. Those differences do not mean that they cannot find help, but it may mean that they will have to compromise, go to a counselor who is more comfortable for one, search for a counselor who can accommodate their differences, or go to separate counselors.

Support Groups with Dissimilar Others

Couples who go to support groups can feel disappointed that there are not other people enough like them or whose loss is enough like theirs. That can be especially likely if the couple lives in an area where few people have had children die or if there is something unusual about their situation or their child's death.

Inadequate Counseling Benefits from an Employer

Counseling is available in many places in the United States to anybody, regardless of their financial situation. But sometimes people must rely on benefits through an employer, and sometimes the counseling provided by those benefits puts them with an inadequate counselor or denies them enough sessions to deal adequately with their problems.

Unhelpful Counselors

Sometimes couples feel that a counselor does not understand them or offers bad advice. I have talked with a number of couples who found the first counselor they saw to be unhelpful, to offer offensive advice, to be a bad listener, or to be incapable of dealing with a grieving couple. Typically those couples drop out of counseling with that first counselor, but eventually find a counselor who can help them.

Blocks to Seeking Help

Money need not be a block to seeking support group or counseling help. Most support groups are free or charge a nominal fee, while health insurance covers some counseling and support groups. Counseling agencies often have sliding fee scales that take into account the financial situation of clients. But while you probably can find affordable help, there are others barriers besides money to seeking assistance.

Feeling Awful Can Feel Right

One of the blocks to finding help for bereaved parents is that it can seem right to them to feel awful. If you cared about your child, of course you are hurting. To some parents, taking away the pain feels like a diminishing of the immense importance of the child's death. But good counseling and support groups do not take away your memories or feelings. They will honor and respect your needs and wishes while helping you in all sorts of important ways.

Not Having Energy or Time

When couples discuss why they do not go to counseling or a support group, the lack of energy and time often are mentioned. Many people who are not bereaved have the same complaint, and when you add to that the draining effects of grief, it makes perfect sense that some grieving parents would feel they do not have the time and energy to seek help.

If you do reach out for assistance, however, in many instances you will be glad you did. In fact, good counseling and good support-group experiences can energize you and help you to get on top of your life in ways that make it easier to organize time. So an investment of energy and time can bring you more energy and time than you put out.

Discomfort with the Focus of a Support Group

Some people who try a support group discover that the group's focus or mood does not fit them. It might be too negative, too emotional or not emotional enough, too focused on people's story-telling or not open enough to story-telling, too religious or not religious enough. As with trying different counselors, some people attend various support groups until they find one that feels right.

Wanting a Helper with a Loss Like Your Own

Some people feel they will benefit more if the helper has had a loss like theirs. They search for a counselor who has had a child die, and the more similar the counselor's loss is to their own, the more they believe they will get helpful counseling. I understand that, but I also think experienced counselors can do a wonderful job of connecting with you even without having endured the same type of loss.

Similarly, some people want a support group of individuals who have suffered losses like theirs. That makes a lot of sense, but I also think well-run support groups with enough empathic members will be helpful even if there are big differences between you and them.

Feeling You Should Tough It Out on Your Own

Some people–more men than women–believe they should solve their own problems and live with their pain without help from others. But even people raised in families with values that say "tough it out on your own" can find going to a counselor or a support group to be very helpful.

We live in a time in which all of us go to experts – for example, dentists, physicians, auto mechanics, plumbers, and travel agents. So rather than thinking of going to a counselor as a confession of weakness or insanity, I think of it as just going to another expert. I can't take out my own appendix or repair my own broken tooth, so why should I try to heal things in myself or my relationships that I cannot heal when there are professionals with the skills to do it?

Al: In the olden days, you didn't go see a counselor. There was something wrong with you if you had to go get counseling. You worked it out in your own manner, and you lived with it.

Barb: I think people still kind of think like that. They kind of look at you like, "My God, and *you* went to see a counselor?" Just like, "Tsk, you must have a screw loose."

Al: I know from talking to older people, like my parents and her parents, I don't think that they thought probably too well of us as far as going to a counselor, until after we'd gone through it. And I think that everybody that knew we went to a counselor, they just accepted it. I didn't care whether anybody understood. I wanted that counseling, and I needed it. And I think she needed it.

Barb: Oh definitely. I think we both did.

Al: I'm sure glad I went, glad we spent the money.

More women than men may seek counseling or a support group and stay with it. They may be more willing than men to seek help, more open to accepting it, more willing to talk about their pain, and more willing to cry in front of others. However, men who became involved often feel that getting help was the right thing to do.

Fearing You Will Be Bullied

Some people do not seek counseling or a support group because they fear being required to think or feel in certain ways. One woman who was pushed hard to enter counseling initially resented the pressue and hated being there. Part of her concern was that she already was feeling pushed around, but eventually she came to value and benefit from the counseling.

Louise: I was told I had to go. I wasn't being given a choice here. I was very depressed, and I wasn't about to discuss anything with anybody. I was gonna deal with it myself, and in *my* mind, I couldn't see any sense discussing it, because he was dead. No amount of discussing was gonna bring him back, so why even discuss it? Why bring all this up? I'll take care of it myself. And Wayne said, "You *have* to come with me to the office. The counselor's gonna be there," and I absolutely refused to go. And he said, "Either you come, or I'm gonna lose my job. That's the way it is." And so I remember going there, *so* angry, and you sat down in this room (laughing) like a three-year-old, and the grief counselor and Wayne's boss and a co-worker were all in there. I felt like I was to blame for his problems at work, and if we didn't get counseling he was gonna lose his job, and that was gonna be my fault. I remember going to see (chuckling) this counselor and sitting there, several times with her, just staring at her, absolutely refusing to talk. I finally started talking to her. And we'd go together, and then she'd see us each separately, for well over a year.

Wayne: The lady was a good counselor.

The Search for Good Support or Good Counseling

Even professionals who seem capable of providing assistance may be amateur at helping bereaved parents, or they may be able to aid some parents but not others, so finding good help can be challenging.The following story is an extreme example, but it illustrates how the first professional helper you go to may not work out well.

Molly: I remember sitting in front of the pastor's desk and he said, "Tell me what happened?" I was sobbing and telling him about it. I look up at him and he's got his face buried in his hands, and he's crying just as loud as I'm crying. I got up and I went and put my arm around him, and I patted him on the back and I said, "I'm so sorry that you lost your son," and he told me what happened to him. And he's crying, and he was telling me all these things. I pulled my chair next to his, sitting there patting him on the back while he talked to me (she laughs). And he told me all this stuff, so we had about an hour and a half of counseling, and I didn't say anything (she laughs). I don't know if Earl remembers it or not, but I remember when he came to pick me up I came outside and Earl said, "Well, how did it go?" And I said, "Oh, he'll be fine" (she laughs). I never went back.

Molly said that in some ways the advice she received from her mother was most valuable of all, but Molly also eventually did find competent counseling–help that gave her valuable resources in dealing with her grief-related problems. You may be referred to good professional help by friends, physicians, nurses, hospital social workers, funeral directors, the clergy, county social services, the school nurse, the telephone book, a community referral service, or the police or sheriff's department.

Potential Risks When Only One Partner Is Involved

In some couples, only one partner goes to counseling or attends a support group. When the partner who does not attend makes it seem there is something wrong with that decision, it can create resentment by the person who goes and make it harder to deal as a couple with relationship issues and the loss.

When both partners do not go for counseling or to a support group, one may change while the other does not. The one who changes may influence the other, or the changes may not be at all a challenge to the other or the relationship. But sometimes when one changes and the other does not, they may become less compatible in ways that are difficult or that challenge the continued existence of the relationship. Similarly, when partners go to different counselors or support groups, they both may change but in ways that do not fit together well and could make working together on issues that one has with the other more challenging.

I do not think it is usually a mistake for one of you to go to counseling or a support group and the other not, for one of you to be more involved than the other, or for the two of you to go to different sources of help. But I think you need to be alert to how the two of you may be drawing apart in these situations. As always, I think the key to heading off problems is the ability to communicate—to talk over how you feel, what you are thinking, and where you want to go. You do not have to say it all, but being in good contact with each other again and again can help a lot. And if you have trouble communicating, I think you would benefit as a couple from finding counseling or a support group that provides a safe and supportive place for you to work together on communicating better.

11

"Medicating"

"Medicating" in Grief

EVERY BEREAVED PARENT tries at times to get away from the pain, disorganization, depression, confusion, and lines of thought connected to the child's death. Many parents do what I call "medicating" in their grief, doing or taking things that block thoughts or numb feelings. The "medication" can be legal or illegal drugs, television, alcohol, food, work, sleep, religion, reading, volunteering, physical effort, sex, or any of a million other things.

Paul: Do you think your drinking changed after he died?

Nick: I started again heavily, but I didn't drink hard stuff. It was just beer, but you still get drunk on beer. Yeah, things got worse again.

* * * * *

Joan: I guess that was kinda my escape, push myself into work or sleeping as much as I could.

* * * * *

Rosa: I smoked pot for a while. I can remember talking to my grief therapist about it, and he sort of said, "Well, probably better for you than Valium." We didn't drink excessively for us. Drinking would be two glasses of wine with dinner on Friday night. For Henry it would be working. I put on weight, probably about forty pounds. So if you consider food numbing, I would think that would be it. It was hard to watch a baby starve to death. And I know, like when I think about Wendy dying and get upset, the first thing I do is go and eat.

* * * * *

Ted: Work is an escape for me.

Amy: I wasn't working. That's where I felt the biggest difference, because he could go to work, he could be occupied. I had an empty house. And I didn't know what I was going to do. Somebody hired me; I worked at a gourmet deli. It was kind of a mindless deal. But it was a fun atmosphere, and that was an escape for me.

For some parents, the choices of "medications" are limited because certain "medications" seem wrong when what is being blocked out is grief over a child's dying. It is hard for them to medicate in a way that seems to deny the seriousness of the child's death. For example, some parents cannot turn to television in order to escape, because television seems foolish in comparison to the seriousness of their child's death. Similarly, for some parents the meanings of alcohol (perhaps happy-go-lucky fun with friends) make it unacceptable as a "medication."

While some parents want to mute their feelings of grief with "medication," others reject this option precisely for that reason. For example, some parents are glad to be helped by antidepressant prescription medications, but others do not like the way that antidepressants mute grief feelings. For them it is important to feel the full intensity of their child's loss.

"Medicating" and How You Get Along as a Couple

Some couples get into conflict because one "medicates" feelings of grief while the other one thinks that is wrong. One spouse might resent the other's "medicating" for all sorts of reasons–maybe because of thinking that emotions should be felt or because of feeling overloaded with responsibilities because of the partner's "medicating." Kathy, for example, talked about how much she was overburdened with child care and the work of the home because Karl had thrown himself into his hobbies and other interests.

> *Kathy:* That's one reason I did everything for the kids. He wasn't around. You can say what you want, but you retreated to your work room or whatever. We didn't even know you were in the house. And so I took over then.

"Medicating" cuts down on how much some couples talk about the loss. That might be what some partners want, in order to avoid dealing with too much too soon or to avoid making their spouse listen to them talk again and again about the loss. Amy discussed the effect of her increased drinking and marijuana use.

> *Amy:* Both those drugs are depressants, and I was depressed. Maybe I could have handled it differently, but then again I don't how much he and I could talk over the same thing over and over and over and over and over again. I think maybe in a way that it gave me a break in talking to him, that instead of talking to him I had a drink or smoked a joint or both.

Bruce described running as a way to "medicate" his grief and to get away from Sally's talking so much about her parents and sisters-in-law.

Bruce: Running was very important to me. It always has been. It was very difficult to run when I was depressed and my wife was in bad shape. But, boy, when I ran it was so mind clearing. I'd run five, six days a week, thirty or thirty-five miles a week. It was great to get away from Sally and her complaints about her family. Now when I speak at grief groups I recommend regular exercise for bereaved men.

Some couples disagree intensely about whether medicating is going on, or if it is going, how much it is going on or how much of a problem it is. So this chapter is about something you and your partner may not even agree exists or is a problem. Regardless of how you view this issue, however, I think the ideas in this chapter may help.

Sometimes, when couples have strong conflicts over "medication" issues, it is hard to tell how much is linked to grief and how much involves a long history of "medication," family patterns of chemical use, power battles over who controls whose life, or money issues. What might seem like a battle that began after a child's death actually may be a struggle that was going on long before the child died. So to understand what is going on between you and your partner, you might have to think not only about grief but also about long-standing patterns, family loyalties, power battles over freedom versus control, and money.

I think a key reason "medicating" can be such an explosive issue is that the critical partner can perceive it as a matter of choice. The resulting problems are especially difficult to deal with when the partner who "medicates" feels that stopping is beyond her or his willpower, while the other believes that a person who medicates can choose not to. To illustrate, the following is a small part of a long argument, with both partners angry and hurt, she crying, and he speaking loudly.

George: I found it hard to believe, what we've been through that you would choose to ...

Steph: I would think it would be the other way around. How could you find it hard to be*lieve* that with what we've been through that I would choose that route?

George: Choose not to work harder at staying sober, because I know that the key to recovery is abstinence.

Steph: Recovery of what? (*George:* alcoholism) Nils' death? (*George:* alcoholism) No, you're *talking* about when I just told, I had told you that (*George:* You had a problem with alcohol). Yes. (*George:* Yeah.) And you can't believe why I wouldn't, after what we just went through that you couldn't believe why I went that way?

George: In the sense that losing a child is a bad thing. Alcoholism is too a bad thing. It's not as bad probably as losing a child. We didn't have any control over losing Nils. That's something that happened, but alcoholism, I recognize, too, that it is a disease. But it is a kind of a thing that a person can really, if they can find inner reserve that they can (three-second pause) kind of cure themself. They can get on the road to recovery. They do have a choice. I give you all the credit in the world for trying hard of late. I found it particularly difficult at that point, when we're trying to essentially start over again. We got the new house. We're still trying to work with our surviving son, and income is important, and you're inebriating yourself, and I couldn't relate to that. I'd ask, "Why would she do that to herself?"

Their intense arguing over her use of alcohol was ongoing, and, as you can see, was entangled in his sense that she could choose to stop.

When conflicts arise, it seems to me that one spouse is usually quite concerned that the other not "medicate" to the point where the spouse or the relationship is badly damaged. Despite the sincerity of this fear, trying to limit or stop another's "medicating" is never easy, especially when the "medication" is something legitimate and even valued in our society, like religion or work.

Lisa: I wanted to know (voice shaking) why Nick felt the way he did about God, and Father Peter told me he's using Him as a crutch. He says that's what happens in many cases. Some people go to the bottle, drugs, God. And that's what he told me, "If you're mad, you have every right to be mad at God." And this is a priest telling *me* that.

I think that the "medicating" in grief often will decrease with time, though the time may seem much too long for a partner impatient to have it end. As with any touchy issue, bringing it up in a way that gets through to the partner is challenging. If you are concerned about a partner's "medicating," it may help if you are clear to your partner about your feelings and try to document why you think it is a problem. ("On this day I observed this, and it had this consequence; on that day, I observed that, and it had that consequence.") At the same time, you must be open to your spouse having a very different view. Your spouse might not see things the same way or might be too invested in medicating at present to be anything but defensive. Being honest with each other is not a bad thing, even if it is frustrating to both of you that your viewpoints are so different.

Sometimes it can help to avoid casting the issue as one person being good and the other being bad. There may be ways that each of you can change to please the other, and then it's not an argument over whether someone is bad, but a discussion of a mutually beneficial trade. For example, I'll watch less television if you cut back how much beer you drink.

If you want help with problem usage of alcohol or drugs, this is so common a behavior that you probably can find help almost anywhere you live. The most common treatment approach is that used by Alcoholics Anonymous and other twelve-step programs. Almost any human service agency or clinic either has a program or can direct you to one. Many treatment programs also have support groups for spouses (and even children) of people with chemical dependency problems. Getting along as a couple is hard enough after a child dies, and adding chemical dependency issues will, I think, almost always make things harder. It can block honesty with yourself and your partner, make communication as a couple more difficult, complicate issues of helping each other and being helped, increase the chances of physical abuse, put health and safety at greater risk, add to financial problems, and put at least the family member or members who are using (and maybe everyone else) in a place where they are less able to deal with the emotions and thoughts of grief.

12

Depression and Your Marriage

YOU OR YOUR SPOUSE may be depressed for long periods. With depression may come feelings of being in a deep and inescapable emotional pit, of lacking energy, and of finding little, if any, interest in anything. There will be feelings of having no purpose or direction and perhaps, at times, a sense that there is no point in continuing to live.

Brett: It was like the worst two years that I have ever gone through. I don't know why it had the hold on me that it did. I don't know if it was 'cause it was my son. I don't know if was 'cause I made, we made the decision to take him off the life support, or 'cause it was the first time I lost the ability to control things, but it devastated me.

Depression colors everything. When a person is depressed, nothing seems to go well.

Al: When you go through something like this, if something else happens, you know it's not true, but it seems like in your mind that everything is going wrong, and it takes you a long time... I'm still getting over it. You'll never totally get over it, but I'm still learning to handle different things, and after a while you realize that everything's not totally against you. It's just life, but you're so damn down.

There are many ways of feeling and acting that can be labeled "depression." Some experts say the depression of bereavement usually is less dangerous and more easily self-corrected than a depression that grinds on and on, that involves deep feelings of self-condemnation, and that has bio-chemical or genetic roots. So if you seem to be experiencing "depression," you may decide while reading this chapter that your depression is not as heavy as some of what I write about here, or you may decide it is even more serious than some of what I discuss and requires prompt medical attention.

Depression and Being Cut Off from Others

Depression often cuts a person off from others and creates a sense of isolation that can lead to resentment that others are not helping and seem so distant. A depressed person may not want to be with people, avoiding them, finding what others say to be irrelevant, and having little interest or energy for deep or prolonged conversation.

> *Hannah:* It was really difficult for me to let people in, because I didn't want to let somebody else down. And I was so far in the pits.

Being the partner of someone who is depressed is hard work and can be very discouraging. The nondepressed part-ner may have to shoulder much of the practical and emo-tional work around the house that the depressed partner would normally do. The partner who is not depressed may feel the marriage provides little or no companionship and may feel pushed away or even treated disrespectfully whenever she or he tries to be helpful. It can be depressing living with someone who is depressed.

> *Lisa:* His moods made me depressed. And I'd get crabby, but I kept saying, "I got to keep goin'. Someone has to keep this goin', 'cause if *I* go, that's it." I was livin' for the kids. I didn't wanta just let them go. I wanted them to have a life. But livin' with a depressed person is *very* depressing. It seems like there's no way out. The more you want to help 'im, the more you get kicked.

At times depression can feel to the depressed person like a downward spiral that cannot be escaped. In the couple relationship, there also can be a downward spiral of distancing. For example, a depressed parent may distance the partner so as not to drag her or him down further or because of wanting to be left alone. This distancing increases the isolation of both parents and can produce a feeling that their marriage is an empty shell. (I do not think it usually is an empty shell, however, because there is still a lot of connection between the partners. But the partners may feel, when there is a lot of distancing, that the marriage is empty.)

Depression as Loyalty to the Child Who Died

Depression can be a form of loyalty to the child who died, as bereaved parents can feel as though it would be disloyal to give up being depressed. As a result, a depressed parent can be upset with the other for not being depressed or for trying to help the depressed parent escape that feeling.

Depression also might be a form of loyalty if the child committed suicide. That probably would not be the only reason for depression, but depression can be an effort to understand the child and to feel what the child felt. In the example that follows, one hint that depression might reflect loyalty to a child who committed suicide is that the woman used her own experience of depression to talk about what she thought was going on with her son just before he killed himself.

> *Hannah:* In December, I went into the hospital, and I was very suicidal. I ended up having shock treatments. I don't think that anybody can be held responsible for a suicide, 'cause I don't really think that you're able to make a decision, *I* wasn't, and I'm assuming Tyler was the same, not able to make a decision. You can't see, I couldn't see, any other way out. That's all you can see is that you know that's gonna end (crying) your pain and suffering. And people say it's selfish. I don't believe it is selfish. I just don't think they are able to see any other way out. And maybe I'm just too defensive, because it's my son, but I just know that when I was suicidal it was like it's the worst, I can't imagine anything (crying) worse, in the world.

Fearing that a Spouse May Commit Suicide

If the parents I have interviewed are typical, thoughts of suicide among bereaved parents are so common they could be called normal.

I would not assume, however, that a spouse who seems to be thinking about suicide intends to follow through. Sometimes words that sound as though they are about suicide are not. For example, a partner who says there seems no point to continuing to live actually may be saying, "I don't want to live like this, with this pain and emptiness" rather than contemplating suicide. Or maybe the person is saying that there is no point to continuing to live but is quite willing to continue. A partner who talks about feeling so depressed that he or she has thoughts of suicide may be saying, "The pain of losing our child is incredible." In short, words that seem to be about suicide may not actually be about a suicide that is likely to happen anytime soon. But I also would not assume that they do not have that meaning. I recommend asking a partner about what she or he is thinking and intending to do, asking a number of times, asking for more clarity, and not taking what is said as the final statement on where your partner will be later today, next week, or in a month.

For most people, a partner's talk about suicide is too scary to be ignored. In writing this, I want to be certain that you take the possibility of suicide very seriously if you have any reason at all to think it is a possibility. This is an area where we want no mistakes. You can hear the concern about making such an error when bereaved parents talk about a time when a partner seemed to be possibly suicidal. The word "suicide" is not always used in these discussions, but it can be read between the lines.

> *Erika:* All I remember is in the first week, he didn't want to leave me. And I don't know if you didn't think you could trust me. Or if you thought I had to have you there.
>
> *Chad:* Well, I just, I don't know, I was very, very worried about Erika. *Really*, really worried.

It is a tremendous additional burden to feel that a spouse's depression may lead to a suicide attempt.

> *Sue:* He was going through a humongous depression; he was *really* depressed. And I was at a loss, personally, what to do. Our communication, whatever I tried, didn't work. It only made it worse. Nothing I did

made any difference. I was scared he was going to commit suicide. I talked to people about that. And the reason I was thinking of leaving him at that time, but he left first, was because I thought it might create a crisis. I was at a loss for what to do. And somebody that was helping me with this just said, "You're going to have to do something here." Everything I was doing wasn't working, so I thought, "Maybe I'll just leave. I can't keep going like this."

Unfortunately, there are no guarantees that you can head off suicide, as a person who talks about it may someday act on those words. While the person's words should be taken seriously, it is impossible to control somebody else's life.

Barb: I talked to the grief therapist about Al's talk of killing himself, because that's all we talked about. It's callous to say, but you got to the point where you think, "Okay, damn it, do it. Just leave me alone." I had called and talked to the therapist, and she said, "Forget it. If he's going to do it, he's going to do it, and there's nothing you can do about it. If he does, you're not at blame. There's nothing you can do for him. He's got to do that himself."

A person who is determined to commit suicide almost certainly can. Still, there is much you can do to help a partner who seems to be considering this act, and one thing is to acknowledge what you are being told. Do not deny to yourself or to your partner that you are hearing words about suicide or hints about it. Another is to ask your partner to tell you more. This gives you a chance to learn more, and it gives your partner a chance to be heard out, to have feelings and thoughts known by you, and to try various ways of thinking. By talking, your partner may change how she or he thinks and feels. And by asking for clarification, you may change things for the better. For example, if your partner is saying, "I don't want to live," a reply like, "Do you mean you don't want to live like this, with this pain and emptiness?" may open the door to new lines of thinking for your partner.

I also think it may be useful to lay out your case against suicide, your own wish for your partner to stay alive, the ways a suicide will add to the pain of those already hurting, how the others will miss the person emotionally and materially, and the life experiences yet to be had. I think it also is important to underscore the reality that almost everybody who is deeply depressed eventually gets through to a non-depressed place—a place where hopelessness is replaced by hope, unbearable pain becomes something more bearable, and suicide no longer seems logical.

Some people have told me about making a difference by offering the partner help in getting to a counselor, a psychiatrist who can prescribe antidepressant medicines, a suicide-prevention hot line, or some other professional help. Since depressed people can have trouble motivating themselves to act, that may mean you will have to search for good professional help. You may even have to make the first appointment and get your spouse there. Remember, help can make a difference. Quite a few grieving parents have told me that they have benefited from being on antidepressant medications or counseling.

Al: I've told a lot of people I've been in counseling, and I say, "Hey, I don't give a damn whether you understand it, like it, or whether you don't. I'll tell anybody, hell, the way I felt about it and the way I feel right now I probably wouldn't be alive here today if I hadn't went to see a counselor. I'd a killed myself. I hurt so."

Some parents find their own way out of depression. Sometimes it just happens, but sometimes it happens after they decide they have reasons to live. The reasons may be things they want to do and experiences they want to have, and often the reasons include other people. They talk about people toward whom they feel caring or responsible, people they love, people they enjoy—for example, spouse, siblings, parents, close friends, or surviving children.

> *Louise:* It was like a month after Will died, and I was *extremely* depressed. (crying) And I was making corn, which was his favorite vegetable. And I had looked at this huge package of corn. I just thought, "Why am I making all this corn? We don't have Will," and I threw it all down the disposal and sat and cried (still crying). I was about as low as I got. I just thought, "If I could just die today I'd be happy" (still crying). But I knew I had these kids I have to take care of, and so I just thought that, "I gotta get through this." I'd get up in the morning and I just couldn't see a whole lot of reason to get through the day. If it weren't for the fact that I have kids. I'd look at them, and I'd think, "Well, I guess for them I have to go on."

I also have talked to people who, in the depth of depression, decided to go on with life just because they trusted that if they continued to live they would make a difference for good in other people's lives. Every life has a potential importance that we cannot know about, and some people trust that if they continue to live they will be able to do good. In fact, some resolve to do so in specific ways, for example, by becoming active in organizations (such as Mothers Against Drunk Driving or a local hospice program) or by becoming involved in some other activity that has a special meaning to them.

I think people seriously considering suicide may benefit from knowing how depression colors everything–past, present, and future–so that life may not seem worth living. But many, many depressed people get past that (on their own, with counseling, or with antidepressants) and are glad that they did not commit suicide. As depression eases, there is reason to live and more joy and hope in viewing past, present, and future. The death remains, but the parent can reach a different relationship with the death and with the child who died.

If your partner seems to be thinking of suicide, it might be helpful to remove obvious means, particularly those your partner gives evidence of thinking about. Get guns out of the house, and have a friend lock them up. Dole out prescription and over-the-counter medications (even aspirin) rather than leaving full bottles around. Keep the car keys in your possession. Watch alcohol and other chemical use, because suicide attempts are more likely with chemical use.

Be clear to your partner about your own desire to live. Don't let your partner guess wrong that with both of you grieving, a murder-suicide is just the thing. Make clear that it would not be doing you a favor to kill you.

I also think that a person who thinks about suicide may be taking a necessary step toward becoming recommitted to life. For some people, it seems almost necessary that they review whether their life is worth continuing and think seriously about ending it before they decide that life *is* worth living. For a long time they may be in an extended limbo where they are not consistently sure that life is worthwhile, but if we could somehow take away their thoughts about suicide, they might never reach a position to commit to life fully.

Almost all bereaved parents who think about suicide pull out of their depression. While it might have been easier not to have come so close, many people who have turned their back on suicide seem stronger because of the path they have traveled. For many of them, I think one reason they decide against suicide is that it seems somehow to dishonor the memory of the child. They decide that staying alive and celebrating the child's life are more fitting ways than suicide to give the child's life meaning.

If you are doubting your own will to live, or if your partner's talk about suicide is sounding like a good idea, immediately seek outside help. You may not recognize your own depression and the ways it is leading you down a path you need not travel. Think of depression as an enemy. It can try to kill a person, partly by misleading that individual into thinking there is no other way out, no other path to travel, and no other way of thinking and feeling. Depression is an enemy that can be fought. It can be fought alone or fought with the help of others. And it can be beaten.

I have tried in the preceding discussion to lay out what I have learned and what I believe to be true about suicide. But a few pages in a book are no substitute for professional help. I hope the perspectives and ideas here can help, if you need help about suicide, but a professional can do all sorts of things I do not even touch on.

Depression that Never Quite Ends

Just as grief may never totally end, a parent's depression connected to a child's death may never totally end. The story did not have a happy ending; something horrible happened that can never be corrected. What some bereaved parents can hope for is to escape depression some of the time or to become less depressed.

> *Nick:* I *have* changed. I know I have. I know I've gotten better. I was down on the bottom, and I know I

couldn't have gotten any further down. I know I'm at least three-fourths of the way up now. I probably will never run another hundred percent like I used to, but it's all right. The rest of my life will be different. It ain't never gonna be the same like it's supposed to have been. But what is it supposed to have been?

But depression also can become a familiar and almost comfortable way of life, a familiar way of feeling, a familiar lens for looking at the world.

Hannah: You get so comfortable being sad that it's sort of hard to be happy. And I think the same thing with the depression. You get so comfortable, because you know how to deal with it, you know how to act when you're depressed, that when things start going right it's kind of hard, because you don't remember how to act.

Some people think of depression as being a failing or a weakness. They are wrong. I have met too many individuals who have come through their depression as strong and good people with a real appreciation for what life has to offer. Sometimes, too, there is a kind of honesty that can come with depression that can be a wonderful gift. So I never think of depression as a failing or a weakness. I think of it more as one way to truth, a way that can be very hard but that eventually can bring one to a higher level of strength and wisdom.

13

Your Couple Relationship with Your Child Who Died

Continuing to Have a Relationship with the Child

MANY BEREAVED PARENTS continue their relationship with the child who died by talking about the child, looking at pictures, cherishing mementos, and continuing to think about the child.

Joan: We talk about him all the time. Our boys always say, "Alex is with us. He's in our hearts." And we've got pictures of him all over. We have his Christmas stocking. When we first put it up, I thought, "Well, we should write a letter every Christmas and put it in his stocking." I did it for the first two years, and then didn't do it, and then this year I wrote another letter. It was kind of fun to go back and look at those letters. We've got a chest in the bedroom, and it's got all his stuff in it, mainly from the hospital.

Brett: We talked about things as far as, like this is for Alex from the nurses. And we have mementoes.

Joan: We have a family picnic every year on his birthday, and I make a birthday cake and decorate it. We let balloons go with a card and roses.

Talk about the child might be not only about keeping the child part of your life but also about keeping the child part of the lives of others–particularly of other children in the family.

> *Joy:* We talk about Jenny a lot. We tell the other kids things Jenny did. In fact, our youngest having chicken pox helped me remember when Jenny had chicken pox, and I was able to tell her, "When Jenny had chicken pox, she wasn't as sick as you are. She got up and got dressed every day. And one day we took a bus to Granny's."
>
> *Stan:* Yeah, we still have pictures, and we want our other kids to know her.
>
> *Joy:* One thing that was really important to us was helping her brother keep the memories he had of her alive. Because he was only three and a half. They were such good friends that I really wanted him to not lose that special relationship they had. And we were lucky enough to record their voices on tape. So we have her voice on tape that we can play for the other kids. In fact, we have her singing happy birthday to her brother, and we'll play that on his birthday. We really feel like the other kids have gotten to know her, and we feel like that's important.

How Many Children Do You Have?

For some parents, part of continuing their relationship with the child is that when telling others how many children they have, they include the child who died in the total. This also is one of the many areas of couple difference. In some couples, partners differ in how many children they tell others they have.

Joy: When people ask us how many kids we have, I always say five, and Stan always says four. It's just that I have to validate her, and that's how, and a lot of times I'll just say we have four here and one in heaven, and that's as far as it will go. I can't say four because we have five. And for Stan it's okay for him to say four, but for me that's just not okay. I don't know if he finds it harder to talk about than I do. And I don't know if that's a guy thing or if that's just the way Stan was. I don't know if some guys *would* talk about it more. I've talked to other people who have lost children, and they say their husbands do the same thing; they don't mention. Sometimes that really hurts me, when he doesn't acknowledge Jenny, and he knows if I'm with him, I'll always give him a evil eye (chuckles). To me that's almost a betrayal, to not acknowledge her. But if that's what he needs to do (laughs), but it bugs me.

Don't be surprised if this is a difference for you and your partner, a difference to tolerate or to talk through.

Seeing and Talking with the Child

Sometimes continuing contact with a child who has died involves seeing or talking with the child. Some parents feel that the child has communicated with them through things that happened. For some couples, those kinds of contacts are very much a shared experience that they understand in the same way.

Chad: We buried him out in the country down here, and, as they were doing the final thing in the casket, a pine cone falls off the tree and lands in the casket. And I told the kids that were pall bearers, "You got an angel

up there watching you, and he's already throwing rocks
down, trying to trick you a little bit."

Erika: We have the pine cone over on the mantle.
We all broke out laughing.

Chad: It's exactly what David would do. He'd be sitting there throwing something in along with.

* * * * *

Rosa: I *really* had a strong sense of Wendy after she
died. There was a book that she had that when you
opened it, it would play music. And after Wendy died,
we just shut the door on her bedroom. We didn't go in
it. It was just shut. But every now and then, the music
would play, with nobody in it. And for a while it was
sort of freaking us out, and then we said, "No, there's
something there," and you could feel a presence. You
could still smell her in that house.

In some couples, though, partners differ in ways that create hard feelings at times. A partner who does not feel in contact with the child may be jealous of the partner who does,
partners may disagree about the reality of the contact, or
one partner may feel that the other's doubt interferes with
the contact she or he would otherwise have with the child.
So here is another area where you should understand that
difficulty can come with the territory, and that other couples
have similar problems. And it is something to be discussed
and perhaps to be talked through until both of you feel okay
about what is going on.

Relationship to the Child's Grave or Ashes

Many parents stay in contact with the child's burial place
or the child's ashes. For some couples, there are big differences in that, for example, one partner might never go

to the cemetery, while the other visits regularly. That difference might not be a problem, but it also may produce hard feelings if, for example, a partner who rarely or never goes feels jealous of the one who does or believes the one who does feels a kind of secret superiority. Conversely, the partner who goes often to the cemetery may wonder if the one who does not really cares about the child who died. But understand that such differences and feelings are normal. Talk them through and expect them to be less difficult with time.

Relationship Through Things
that Were the Child's

For most parents, continuing contact with a child who died includes contact with things that were part of the child's life. For example, some parents keep clothing and toys of the child and take them out now and then to look at and touch. Photos or videos also are a way to keep in contact with the child.

You and your spouse may both treasure things, but you may also find yourselves in conflict, the most common being that one of you may want to get rid of things or at least put them out of sight more than the other. For one of you, the things may be precious reminders. For the other, they may bring back sharp pain and make it more difficult to control emotions; or it may seem like the things make you live too much in the past and not enough in the present.

If you have conflict in this area, you will be like many other couples. And these are matters that, I think, are relatively easy to compromise about. For example, photos or the child's things can be limited to certain areas of the house or can be limited in the quantity that are out.

Long-Term Relationship with the Child

Agreeing on Your Relationship with the Child

Couples often reach agreement about the basics of their long- term relationship with the dead child. For example, you might agree about whether to have pictures up, what pictures to have up, and how to relate to the pictures. You also may agree about things to do as a couple that remember or honor the child.

> *Sue:* It's not a ritual but we do look at pictures of her. We'll buy flowers in her memory. There's certain things we have done in her name, for instance giving something to somebody as a memory of her, which is kind of a healthy way of remembering her.
>
> *Gabe:* We do it anonymously, like it'll be "in memory of loved ones that have died."

Some parents have strong desires to be reunited with a child who died. They may have specific images, plans, hopes, expectations, or intentions for reunion.

> *Denny:* When we get up in heaven, they'll be waiting for us. We'll be eighty years old, and we'll have babies up there waiting for us, so then maybe we'll be luckier that way. That's the only thing that gives us any kind of solace.

With shared plans to reunite in heaven, you probably will decide to work as a couple on what you believe will ensure that reunion in heaven will happen. That probably means you will agree about morality and religious activity and beliefs.

> *Stan:* Jenny's brought us closer to really searching to find out what the truth is, 'cause we believe that there's an afterlife and that Jenny is in heaven now and,

boy, we want to see her, so we had to know how to get there (laughs). So we became much stronger religiously. And that's one of the reasons why we changed churches, because we really didn't feel that the church we had been going to was teaching in the right direction. You find comfort in knowing that there's a God who cares for you and we're going to spend eternity together, and we'll have Jenny for eternity.

Tracking the Child's Timeline

Another part of maintaining a long-term relationship with a dead child is to continue to track the child along what would be the child's timeline. Some parents wonder repeatedly, as the months and years pass, what the child would be like.

> *Rosa:* Every now and then when I'm shopping I still go through the girls' department, think, "If Wendy was alive, what size would she be? A ten-year-old will wear a size twelve, and what would I buy for her?"

Some parents look at others who are the age the child would be now to get a sense of what the child would be like. Keeping track of the child's timeline can mean feeling pain when points are reached on the timeline that would have been significant.

> *Louise:* The year that Will would have graduated I remember calling a friend from our support group and said, "How did you handle graduations?" Because he would have graduated; all of his friends were graduating. We were getting announcements from all these people to go to their parties. I wanted to leave town.
> *Wayne:* I went to the parties. (small laugh) I went. She didn't.

Louise: I didn't. Yeah. I said, "How did you handle this? I just can't do this." And she said she couldn't either. So she sent cards out with a letter of explanation. So that's what I did.

If you are like Wayne and Louise, your differences in how you deal with the timeline may not be a problem. You each understand the other and respect your differences. But there are also couples in which each becomes upset with the other about timeline matters. The one who is less emotional may feel impatient with the one who is more emotional. The one who has stronger feelings may feel the other does not care enough about the child or is not supportive enough. Here, too, I think the thing to do is to understand such differences are normal, to tolerate them, and to talk enough so that you can each understand your partner's views.

Continuing Relationship Between Earth and Heaven

Some parents continue their relationship with the dead child by believing the child is in heaven watching over them and the entire family or that the child is a presence somewhere nearby. Some parents continue to parent the child who died by regularly praying for the child's well being.

Jay: We pray a lot for her. I say a prayer every night.
Alice: Now that's another thing. The pastor has asked him, "Why do you pray for her? She doesn't need your prayers." But we do it anyway.

If you are like Jay and Alice, you will agree about your continuing relationship with your child. If you differ, here is another area for accepting that differences occur and for understanding and respecting your differences.

14

Birthing or Adopting
Another Child

Should We or Shouldn't We?

MANY COUPLES who have experienced the death of a child reach a time when they discuss whether to try to have or adopt another child. The issues are complicated.

Some parents feel they could not tolerate another loss or even the anxiety of that possibility. Some women do not want to be pregnant again, and some men do not want to deal with their wife being pregnant. Some parents do not want the burden of caring for another infant.

Sometimes there is a sense that the dead child still is present and will make it impossible for a next child to be genuinely herself or himself.

> *Rosa:* I wanted a baby, and I would have done anything to have it. But I, at that point, had a really strong sense that Wendy's presence was in the house and that if I got pregnant again that it would be Wendy, and that wouldn't look like Wendy, but it would be Wendy, and I would know it's Wendy and she would know it's Wendy. If nobody else would know, it would be sort of

my little secret. It was my way of bringing her back, 'cause you could feel her. You could just feel her presence in the house.

For some couples, deciding to have another child is a choice to go on with life—not to stop grieving, but to have more in life than their sorrow. Sometimes interest in having another child comes out of a feeling of incompleteness and the desire to have a child to parent, and it can be spurred on by a sense of a ticking biological clock.

Some parents say a healthy baby fills emotional gaps created by their child's illness and death, giving a sense of doing things right.

> *Iris:* It was good to have a baby. I remember even after Jeff was born, and they were gonna send him to Children's, thinking, "I want to have another (sad little laugh) baby so I can do this right (laughing) and have a happy ending." It was so hard, because he was at Children's and I was at a different hospital. I didn't want to end it that way. I wanted to have a baby (laughing) the right way.

Some parents who choose to try to have another child talk about having more love to give. For some, a child is a kind of genetic or good-works heritage to pass on to the world. Some parents who decide to have another child say they want a surviving child to have a sibling.

Some parents want a child of a certain gender, either to replace a child who died or to avoid having a new child too entangled in memories of a child no longer alive.

No major decision in life is totally rational. However much you try to know the relevant facts, such decisions are acts of faith and hope, supported by guesses about what may happen. Sometimes the decision to try to have another child is rooted in a sense of not wanting to mark time in life and also in a belief that terrible things could not happen twice in a row.

Sometimes family and friends, fearing the worst, oppose a couple's decision to have another child. There also are couples pushed by family and friends toward fostering or adopting, rather than birthing or having no new child at all.

So one issue you and your spouse may face is whether to try to bring another child into your lives. There may be strong pro and con arguments, and others in your life may have strong feelings about the matter. You can try to be rational, but decisions about having children are never totally rational. Most people would say this is a choice that demands full agreement, that it's not good if one of you decides to have another child when the other does not want one, but I know couples who have gone ahead when only the woman wanted one. My strong recommendation, however, is to talk this through until you are sure you are both in agreement.

Genetic Advice in Making a Decision

If a child died of a condition that could be genetic, without exception, the couples I interviewed who thought they might want to try birthing another child tried to learn the risks of having a child with the same condition. Genetic advice includes an estimate of how likely it is that a next child would have the same condition. Very low probabilities say that, as far as genetics go, it is okay to go ahead, but even probabilities as high as one chance in four may not stop many couples. I think if you have any reason to be concerned about this issue, genetic advice can make your decision about having another child a bit more rational, and it may reduce your fears if you decide to go ahead.

Genetic advice does not always help, though. Kathy and Karl told about the death of a daughter with multiple birth defects. Genetic tests of the daughter and of both parents showed no problems, and they were encouraged to have another child.

> *Kathy:* The doctor said, "This is just a rare occurrence," so we had our next one. And he pretty much had the same thing. He was much smaller than she.
>
> *Karl:* We *had* seen quite a few specialists in between. We were assured that the possibility of it happening again just was not there.

Some couples who consider having another child but are concerned about possible genetics problems are open to amniocentesis, which involves using a needle to draw amniotic fluid out of a pregnant woman's womb. In the fluid will be fetal cells that can be examined for a number of known genetic defects, knowledge that can help couples decide whether to abort the child.

> *Scott:* Amnio is such a relief. It doesn't guarantee anything, but it did definitely guarantee that we weren't gonna have another trisomy 18 baby and any other chromosome abnormalities that they can tell from an amnio.
>
> *Tina:* We did the amnio, and that gave us some peace of mind.

However, amniocentesis can create problems of its own. One couple interviewed felt that amniocentesis caused the complications that ended the pregnancy that followed their child's death.

Becoming Pregnant and Giving Birth

Trying to Become Pregnant

Sometimes the decision to try to have another child is made soon after the death, but some couples and experts suggest waiting at least six months or a year before deciding to try to become pregnant. The wait helps a couple to be a bit more rational about whether pregnancy is a good thing. Perhaps even more important, it is more likely that a pregnancy (and perhaps the parenting of a new child) will not go on while the parents are in deepest grief.

A bereaved couple's feelings and thoughts about a next pregnancy are tangled in feelings and thoughts about the child who died. A next pregnancy is not just a next pregnancy but a pregnancy after a child's death. Because of this, it might end certain anxieties and tensions driven by feelings arising from the death. Some parents talk about a next pregnancy giving hope and joy, though it does not end grieving. However, particularly if a child's death was connected to premature birth or genetic problems, the next pregnancy often involves anxiety about whether this pregnancy too will end prematurely or whether this child will be born with genetic problems. Also, a pregnancy after a previous loss that involved premature birth typically involves intrusive efforts by physicians to minimize the chances of this happening again, perhaps including dreary weeks of required bed rest.

A New Child May or May Not Help You to Heal

Whatever the original reasons for having another child, in my experience most bereaved parents say the next child is in some ways healing.

> **Todd:** He helped a lot. Having him to take up time and require attention just took our minds off the last

major event in our lives. And we had a new major event. You can only focus on so much at a time, and nothing like a baby to demand one hundred percent of your focus. (*Iris:* Yeah. [laughs]), so that was a blessing.

* * * * *

Joy: The Bible says "Blessed are those who mourn for they shall be comforted." And the son we had after Jenny died was our comfort, 'cause he really did bring a lot of happiness back into our home, and that was probably a high, having him be born.

However, a new child does not guarantee a rift in the marital relationship will be healed. Even if you have a new child, you will still have to work on couple communication, tolerating differences, and the other things that can help a couple to achieve a strong and lasting relationship.

Avoiding "Replacing" the Child Who Died

A child who is born after a sibling has died will be compared with the child who is gone.

Todd: When our next child was born, he turned pink right away and cried for the next two hours. They said, he was the loudest (*Iris:* He was a *loud* baby [still laughing]. It was so reassuring.) one. (*Todd* laughs) There's the answer to *our* prayers. (*Iris* still laughing) And it was a nice sound for about two weeks.

Many parents say that they have heard or read that replacing a child who has died is bad for a next child, that a next child has to be her or his own person, not a stand-in for someone else.

I think that usually is not a problem, though. Often it seems that the next child, from the moment of birth, makes clear that she or he is not a replacement. Parents might feel upset that the child is not enough like the child who died but also relieved.

> *Stan:* I was disappointed at first that the baby born after Jenny died wasn't a girl.
>
> *Joy:* We were both disappointed about that. (*Stan:* 'cause we thought we deserved a girl back.) And God had a higher plan. I remember feeling really disappointed when he was born for like maybe the first twelve hours, thinking we wanted this dark-haired little girl and we got this blond-haired little boy. It was like, "Whoa, didn't the message get received or what?" And I guess I realized that what God in his wisdom had given us was perfect for our family because he was totally different. He was a boy. I really feel like our older son needed a brother more than he would have needed a sister, so really, God in his wisdom gave us the perfect baby for our family.

Even if a next child is very different from the one who died, parents still might feel the next child is in some way a replacement.

> *Rosa:* Wendy died June ninth; her brother was born the following year June eleventh. So that was a big thing, 'cause I didn't want him to be born on the anniversary of Wendy's death. It was hard having him that close. I can remember, after he was born, thinking I was betraying Wendy. When he was born, I lost that close feeling to Wendy.

My advice is not to be surprised if a next child, if you have one, at least for a while seems to be in some sense a replacement for the child who died. But also do not be surprised if the new child quickly establishes herself or himself as a very different person.

15

Parenting Together
after a Child Dies

THIS CHAPTER is for couples who have surviving children or who birth, adopt, or foster other children after a child dies. If you and your spouse are parenting or will be parenting other children, you should know that having a child die will affect how you treat other children.

Neglecting Other Children

I am sorry if what follows is hurtful to you, but I think it is true. Many bereaved parents say that for months or even longer after a child dies they have less strength and energy to devote to another child. It is harder to laugh, smile, or be playful. It is harder to focus on a surviving child, and some parents continue to talk about the child who died for months and even years–often so glowingly that their other children feel less important to their parents.

As in other areas of grieving, parents often differ in how much they are available to their other children. Some couples take turns being more tuned in to their children, While in other couples it is always one parent who is more involved while the other is wrapped up in grief and depression. When this is the case, the spouse who is more involved in parenting often resents carrying that load.

Lisa: If I was grieving like you are, if I didn't take care of the kids, who would? You got a sixteen-year-old that you can't just leave, and an eight-year-old. What do you do? I had a tough time tryin' to stay close to the kids, and he wasn't helpin' out. And I'm doin' the discipline, and I'm thinking, "These guys are gonna hate me," and then I kept sayin' in my own head, "They can't, 'cause discipline is a part of love." You gotta discipline.

In some families, with parents seeming to neglect other children, an older child starts parenting younger siblings. Regardless of whether this is a problem in the short run, in the long run I think it usually is. The older child does not have adult wisdom, knowledge, or skills, and younger children will not get everything they need when a sibling replaces parents. Moreover, the sibling who acts like a parent may miss valuable childhood experiences and relationships with siblings.

Maybe you are thinking that neglect should be avoided at all costs, but I believe it is important to be "real" for your children. Even if you could force yourself to act as though a child had not died, it would be an act. Your surviving child or children would sense that, and the pretense would confuse and perhaps even alarm them. They need to know that you grieve, that you have the feelings you do about the child who died. It would be the wrong message to say that having a child die does not matter to you. They need to know that you care, that your children count with you. They also need permission from you for their own grief—about the sibling who died and about other losses they experience, including the loss of you as the parent you would have been.

Although I think it normal for grieving parents to neglect other children, I think that down the road it is a good thing to apologize to children for that neglect. Apologizing is one way to tell your children that they count with you and that you know in some ways they not only lost a sibling, but they also lost their parents for a while.

> *Glenda:* I don't know what people do who have tiny ones and they have to be there and cook, 'cause ours, at least, could fend for themselves. But we sure neglected them. It's like all our energy was focused. We knew they were okay physically. But in the meantime we forgot them mentally. I have apologized to them a couple of times for neglecting them. They didn't say it, but I think we did it, that we were so consumed that we let them go.

Parenting a Child Who Is Grieving

Surviving children must deal with their own feelings of grief. Even children too young to talk may realize that they have lost someone important in their lives.

> *Paula:* He wasn't talking yet. And afterwards he'd go around the house just like he had lost something. He couldn't express his feelings. And I know he was looking for Jerry, because they played together.
> *Paul:* Did you think your older son was affected?
> *Paula:* He was. At the time, he just wanted to be left alone.
> *Pete:* It was a long time before he opened up about it.

The grief that surviving children face involves not only the sibling who died but also their relationship with parents who in their grief have been less available to them.

Joy: I don't know if he really understood everything that was going on. All he knew was that his world was turned upside down and then he had these parents who didn't have any life in 'em, and his best friend was gone, and I'm sure it was just awful for him, too, because he had known Jenny all his life.

Some couples involve surviving children in the funeral planning and ceremonies in ways that help those children to grieve. Many couples try, beyond the funeral, to speak with their surviving children about grief.

Elaine: Our older son probably had the worst time of all of our kids dealing with Kyle's death because they were so close. He held all of his emotions inside. He never cried at the funeral. It was real hard for him 'cause he just really didn't know how, and a lot of it he did to spare us, because he felt if he could keep himself together then it would be easier on his dad and I. I told him one time when I was cutting his hair, "You have to cry. You can't spare Dad's and my feelings." He was in college the next year and he wrote a paper in his English class on if he had ever lost anyone that was close to you. I saved it because that was the first time he had ever really dealt with Kyle's death. They were always after each other and then they'd be out arm in arm, and like he told me one day, "I not only lost my brother, but I lost my very best friend."

You remember the night we sat the kids down and told them that if they expected their life to go back to perfectly normal, then they were never going to be able to heal from this, because our life could never be the same anymore? He was gone, and he was a very big part of it, so it can't be the same. Yes, we will be happy.

Yes, we will laugh. Yes, we will have fun together, but it will always be different. Because a very important part of our family is gone.

Some parents try to help surviving siblings by arranging for counseling checkups or special classes for children who might be grieving. For some children, those steps are very helpful. But despite such efforts, a child may struggle with heavy feelings about the sibling who died even years afterward. Such struggle can be a good thing and developmentally appropriate, but it still can be alarming to parents who are at a different place in their grieving than their child is. My advice is to realize that just as you and your spouse must understand and accept your differences in grieving, you also must understand and accept that a child will mourn the loss in her or his own way.

(Over)Protecting Surviving Children

Many bereaved parents say that they individually or as a couple, at least for a while, overprotect a surviving child.

> *Louise:* I think I became very protective of them at first. I remember, the weeks after Will died, calling the school saying, and I don't know what I was afraid of. (*Wayne:* Their crossing the street or something.) I was afraid of everything. And I remember calling the school saying, "Don't let them go home with anybody. Don't let anybody take them out regardless of what these people say to you." I'm sure the school thought I was real loony.
> *Wayne:* And sleepovers.
> *Louise:* Yeah, I didn't let them sleep over.

What some couples considered overprotection they sometimes saw as a problem, especially when the spouses disagreed. One spouse might be concerned that they were over-protecting a child, or at least that the other spouse was. And the other spouse would think what was going on was totally appropriate. As with other differences in grieving, this is something to discuss and perhaps resolve, but it also may be something simply to be accepted.

> *Gail:* I think we became more protective. I was very scared to let them go out the door and do anything, to go playing.
> *Vince:* That part's not a "we." That part's a "you."
> *Gail:* I said, "*I* was (*Vince:* okay, yeah) very scared to let them go out the door."

Protection issues, like others in grief, can bring a family to counseling. In one family, an older child reacted so strongly to the overprotection that the parents and child entered family counseling.

> *Elaine:* We've been in counseling for almost a year. We worked through a lot of the hurt with her, too, because so much of how we treat her has direct bearing on what has happened. It's just fear that you're going to lose another child.

Parent (over)protectiveness can affect the marital relationship as well. A parent devoting herself or himself to surviving children necessarily has less to give the other parent, a situation that can produce lasting feelings of sorrow for one or both partners.

> *Karl:* To this day, the kids are *number one.* I might be a "four." There is no number two and number three. They're all the kids, and that's truly how she feels. And I understand how she feels (she sniffles). And I don't

really put her down for that. I don't think that that's
necessarily wrong, but it did have an effect on me. And
I think it had an effect on us. But I still feel very strongly
about her, and I know that she feels very strongly about
me. So it's almost like, well, then, you just let that go.
And it maybe is not all that important.

Kathy: Well, I guess, for me, I didn't sweat the small
stuff. My marriage became kind of the small stuff.
(*Karl:* Yeah.) It just wasn't very important to me. I was
hurting so much over everything else that we didn't
seem that important.

Your Surviving Children May "Parent" You

After a child's death, surviving children sometimes enter
into their parents' marital relationship in ways that would
not have occurred if their sibling had not died. Some surviving children, even very young children, provide comfort
to parents that the spouses may be unable to provide one
another. Some surviving children work at protecting their
parents from things such as nosy neighbors, visiting sales
people, or an unhealthy diet. A surviving child also may help
organize bereaved parents, for example, by helping them get
going in the morning or making out grocery shopping lists.

Some family experts say that when children parent their
parents it harms both the family and children. Some parents
feel that the child was better off for the experience, however,
and I am inclined to agree. I think "parenting" a parent is
like doing necessary chores when a parent is unavailable to
do them or like growing up doing a share of the chores that
need to be done. I think it often is just a matter of being a
responsible and productive household member. So from my
perspective, when the parents cannot do the necessary work

or give each other enough help, the help of children seems, up to a point, appropriate. Beyond a certain point, though, I agree with the experts that children who are parental are hurting themselves and maybe everyone else. I'm not sure what that exact point is, but I think no older child should go more than a few weeks and no younger child should go more than a few hours without being able to be a child.

Children Who Give Reason to Go On

For many bereaved couples, the opportunity to parent other children motivates them to stay together and go on with life. I think that is okay, and I also believe children can be aware of how important they are in those ways. That knowledge can color how they relate to their parents, who may find that acknowledging this awareness is one of the tasks they face as parents.

> *Rosa:* Our children say, "Wendy was born sick. Mummy and Daddy were very sad when she died." Our seven-year-old was talking about her just the other day, "Mummy and Daddy were really sad, and then we had me and my brother at the hospital, make Mummy and Daddy happy again." So they are our rays of sunshine that made Mommy and Daddy happy.

I know there are parents who say that a surviving child made the difference between them choosing life over suicide or staying with their spouse rather than divorcing. To the extent that children can sense that they have had such a role, they might feel that they were bearing tremendous responsibility. And those feelings might make them different from their friends. How does a couple parent a child who feels that burden and must deal with being different from friends? I think for many couples in that situation, a key part of parenting is to show appreciation by trying to function as well as possible.

Louise: I'd get up in the morning and I just couldn't see a whole lot of reason to get through the day. If it weren't for the fact that I have kids. I'd look at them, and I'd think, "Well, I guess for them I have to go on." I think if our son who died had been our only child, I really don't think I'd still be alive.

AH: So there were times you felt suicidal?

Wayne: Oh, absolutely!

* * * * *

Elaine: We're very, very fortunate in that we had to put our lives back in order. Because you think, how must our other children feel, if you can't get your life back together. How must they feel? "Are we not worthy enough for you to be able to stop it? Because we're still here, aren't we fulfilling your life enough that you can't get it back together for us?" And that was kinda what brought me around.

16

Staying Together and Getting Along

Divorce

PERHAPS STAYING MARRIED has never been a question for you, as you and your spouse have been committed to each other all along. But if either of you have ever considered divorce following your child's death (or if you're not sure whether your spouse has), I want to say some things to you about this issue.

Despite some old research and the popular belief suggesting this is the case, I do not think convincing evidence exists that divorce is more likely if a child dies. A child's death leads to many things that could push a couple apart, but it also leads to lots of things that push a couple together very strongly.

Some bereaved parents think seriously about divorce or fear that their partner will leave, but I think the roots of that possibility often were present long before the child died. Perhaps there were tensions arising from communication problems, repeated power battles, problems from being too different, personality clashes, chemical dependency, or physical abuse. Many U.S. couples have such problems, and many break up because one or both partners cannot stand to stay in the relationship or because they do not find (or know how to find) enough help in themselves or from outside sources to reduce, neutralize, or live with these problems.

Just as your child's death has changed you forever, it also will have changed your spouse and your marriage. Even if you got along well before, there is a sense of living with someone who is in some ways a stranger. There also is a sense of living in a new relationship, with questions for both of you about whether the new relationship will be satisfying. Just the newness of self, partner, and relationship is enough to make some people wonder whether divorce is possible.

I have heard bereaved parents give dozens of different reasons for not divorcing, but most said they did not want to face additional loss or that the spouse was the one person who could best remember the child.

> *Joy:* Divorce never even came into our thoughts. I guess we figured we have lost enough. Why would you want to lose anymore? And I guess I've always thought that nobody else could ever, ever understand. We can understand each other more than anyone could ever understand. We've been through something together. How can you share that with someone else? To lose a child together, for us it was just like a cementing. We've been through something together that nobody else could ever imagine.

In addition to this sense that the child who died is a bond that holds them together, many parents cite concern for their surviving children or children born after the death as a reason they stay married. They want their children to have two parents.

> *Rosa:* If I hadn't had the kids, I think I would have left him. It was sort of, "I've got two kids and you're nice, you're

kind." He wasn't doing anything mean. He was just (*Henry:* quiet) quiet. He can be so maddening. When he was, you were depressed, he didn't sing; he didn't hum; he didn't have hobbies; he just worked and was quiet.

* * * * *

Kathy: I think a lot of it's our oldest child maybe. We always felt that he deserved two of us at our best.

Karl: Umhm. That's very important to me, that the kids have a mother and father. I think that we both feel and both truly believe that it's important for the kids that we stay together. Children are very important to us, maybe a little bit more so than other people, because we've lost two. We don't want to hurt them.

Some parents also talk about wanting to stay with a spouse who is very needy or hurting. In addition to every-thing else, they do not want to cause more pain or abandon the spouse in a time of need.

I think if you are like many couples, you will find that you and your spouse have too strong a commitment and too much history together to divorce.

Steph: I was sixteen, he was eighteen, when we started going together. It just seems like there's just too many years, too many memories. I mean the memories for Nils are so short. Like four and a half years. Well, for me a little bit more, 'cause I carried him, but hav-ing to give those up (four-second pause), I don't know if I can actually ever give up the other, the good times.

George: I guess we're both quick to forgive each other because we *have* been together for a long time. We both can reflect on the good more so than the bad. We have had our differences, but still Steph is good for me; I'm good for her. We do love each other.

Many parents say that the possibility of divorce motivates them to stay together, though other factors—like their commitment to surviving children and protecting them from further trauma—also are important.

I have not interviewed many bereaved parents who have divorced or are close to divorcing, but I have some impressions about couples who have split up. I think divorce can help one partner, if not both, to escape long-standing intolerable difficulties—for example, emotional abuse, physical abuse, distressingly crazy interactions, or overwhelming feelings of incompatibility. I do not think divorce ends the psychological relationship, however. I believe each partner continues to think and dream about the other and see all sorts of things in life partly in terms of the relationship that has ended. And when the couple has lost a child, those thoughts, dreams, and perspectives are entangled in the experience of the child dying.

For some couples, staying together is as easy as breathing. For others, it is an achievement that requires a lot of work. When I interview bereaved parents, it often is years after the death and by then many couples are getting along much better than they were during the early stages of their grief. What do couples who stay together and achieve a good relationship do? The following are key things that worked for them.

Recognizing and Living with Differences

Getting along as a couple involves recognizing differences and coming to terms with them. Everybody deals with grief differently, and you cannot expect your spouse to deal with it the way you do. You differ in your grieving in numerous ways—including what you think about, what you feel, the timing of your ups and downs, what you do with your feel-

ings, how much you want to talk about things, who you want
to talk with, in what ways you express your feelings, and
how you think about the child.

Some couples struggle because one partner assumes that
the two are alike. Sometimes one or both partners cannot
understand their differences or why the differences exist. A
key part of the grief process as a couple, however, is devel-
oping your awareness that the two of you grieve differently
and making progress toward accepting, perhaps even appre-
ciating, the differences.

Todd: Some of it you just don't understand. It's just
the way it is. You learn that, okay, this is the way she
feels. I don't understand why, but that's the way she
feels, and okay, this is the way I feel. She doesn't know
why, but that's the way I feel, and on the other hand
maybe some of that I can understand. Maybe she
understands better what I feel, and it takes some time.
Sometimes it was things she said and explained to me,
and maybe I still wouldn't understand, but at least I
knew what she said, and it's just one of those things. It
takes time, at least it took me time.

Iris: There's things that have come up recently that
we've talked about and come to understanding of.
Sometimes you almost have to agree to disagree.

Todd: Yeah. Yeah. 'Cause she's different, and I'm different. And we're wired up differently.

Iris: Come from different kinds of backgrounds, and
different personalities.

Todd: And some things will make me a little more
sober and reflective, and other things will trigger her.
And she may not understand why I'm being so quiet or
off somewhere else. But maybe she's learned that, "Hey,

I just want to be left alone with that for a little while." She's the kind that wants to be with somebody when she's feeling bad. I'm not. Just leave me alone.

Iris: I've learned not to take that personally. I figured out that it doesn't have anything to do with me; it's just him (laughs).

In accepting the differences, you also can come to see that there is value and strength in difference. There are ways you will balance each other out and also ways that, because of the differences, you will learn important things about grief and about life from each other. Also, if you seem to take turns being down, having one partner better able to function ensures there is someone to deal with the basics—everything from bringing in income to getting the garbage to the curb.

Learning to Accept and Be Patient with the Grief Process

If you have trouble with your partner's grief, if you feel impatient, you have something to work on to make your marriage go more smoothly. It is important to learn to accept and be patient with the slow, irregular course of mourning.

Bruce: You don't put a time frame around grieving. You can't say grief will last a month, a year, two years. You can't put a time frame around it. You learn to be patient. If your sex life is bad for a year or two or more, you just go on. So we've been very patient with each other.

* * * * *

Jack: We recognize that it's just part of being human. And it's easier to forgive and move on because of that. We understand it better. I would not have understood had *you* lost a child, I met you shortly afterwards, and now I see all these emotions. I would not have understood 'em. I would not have liked 'em. And I would not have stayed with you. Vice versa. Had I been the one that lost a child, bet you my life you probably would not have stayed with me. (*Angela:* Right.) But the fact that we went through it together, we understand *what* it is that is drawing these out. So we can forgive and move on easier.

Acceptance takes many forms, but I think a big part of it is not judging. Sometimes it is a struggle to accept and not judge, but it is a struggle well worth the trouble. When I hear people discuss problems with being judgmental it seems to me that often a big part of accepting the other and the prolonged and irregular process of grieving is to accept yourself. If you do not accept yourself, it is just about impossible to accept anyone else. Do not demand of anyone–including yourself–that grief be a certain way. Just let it be.

Paul: What would be important things you'd want to communicate to other couples who have lost a child?

Brett and Joan: (simultaneously) To be gentle with yourself. (*Joan* laughs)

Joan: Don't let other people's opinions decide how you're gonna grieve or what you're gonna do or how you're gonna feel, 'cause there were times when I felt a certain way, because that's how I thought that I should feel. (*Brett:* Oh, we did that a lot. Remember we'd ask how were we supposed to be reacting?) Yeah.

Brett: What are people thinkin' about us? Like at the funeral, and when we do things, are we doin' it the way we're supposed to? Like we thought there was some answers (*Joan:* a right way and a wrong way) and like even at his wake, we were joking with the nurses and, you know, should we let people see us laughing. We weren't sure if we were doing things the way that was like socially acceptable.

Learning to Go Elsewhere to Have Needs Met

Grieving parents can be very needy. With both spouses grieving, both need an awful lot, and neither may have much to give. It can help your relationship considerably for one or both of you to have friends, relatives, or others willing to listen and provide support.

> *Iris:* I had a couple of friends who were really very supportive. And they let me talk and talk and talk and talk and talk. So, yeah, I did a lot of talking to them. And they both had, not unlimited time, but they had lots of time to listen. So I felt that they helped me get through. I could talk to them about what I couldn't talk to Todd about. We both kind of felt like we needed two hundred percent (laughing), and the other one had zero to give.

* * * * *

> *Rosa:* I think that I'm probably still with Henry because I got a lot of support from my sister. If I hadn't had the support from her, that someone that wanted to know your innermost secrets and how you were feeling, it would have been really, really lonely. Because I need that sort of emotional intimacy.

Time Out

It's not good to go through every moment of life glued to each other. Your relationship benefits at times from one partner getting physical and emotional distance from the other. Sometimes the "time out" is simply room to be alone, to be distracted, to have private thoughts, to relax. A grieving parent may need time away from a partner in order to distance pain or to feel it in full intensity.

Getting distance temporarily does not mean cutting the bonds of help and connection with your spouse. In fact, the opposite is true. Knowing the bonds are there makes it easier to seek temporary distance, and having the distance now and then can make the bonds all the stronger.

Communicate

I think most couples who do well together put considerable effort into communicating, which helps them see eye-to-eye about a lot. It does not make differences go away, but it often makes good things happen despite, or even because of, the differences.

> *Marsha:* I'd say keep the lines of communication open. That's rule number one. Keep talking with one another.

* * * * *

> *Alice:* Talk. I think that's the big thing, talk.

* * * * *

> *Amy:* Talk to each other, and let each other know that it's okay that, "I don't like the way you're grieving right now, or if that's grief, I don't like it. This is the way I'm doing it. I think I'm grieving more than you, and I don't mean to hurt you." As long as you have a safety net to be able to say that to each other, and then maybe the next evening you can say to each other, "Thanks for listening then. I know I might have sounded crazy at that moment, but I needed to say it."

Talking can help you learn what your partner needs and wants and can help your partner to know what you need and want. Talking also can help you to know yourself, which can make your marriage stronger as well.

The keys to communicating are to let yourself know yourself, to be real, to be open about your thoughts and feelings, and to help create a shared situation in which it is safe to be honest. Creating these conditions is not always easy, because as you talk you may touch on many vulnerable areas. One of the biggest is when people talk about responsibility for the death. Be aware that it is a touchy area, one that may require a lot of tact, careful listening, and acknowledgement.

How do you know communication is going well? One sign is that it keeps going on, that neither of you has been shut up. Another sign is that you reach times of shared sorrow and also, down the road, shared laughter.

At the same time, I stand by what I said about communication in chapters 2 and 4. Many couples go through periods of minimal or no communication and that can be okay. Sometimes communication works even if it's only a little bit at a time or only indirect, or one spouse talks and wants to talk much more than the other.

Renewed Commitment to Your Spouse and to Life

I think the couples who succeed at staying together and getting along well typically have reached a place where they have made a commitment to stay married and to live a life that both feel committed to living. Let me emphasize again, however, that the commitment to life does not deny the significance of your child's death. In fact, for many couples this desire to go on is based on the significance of the child's death.

Erika: I think we made a decision at some point that we were going to continue to be married (slightly amused), and that we were going to have to work at it for the other two children.

Chad: Obviously you've got a real strong common bond now, if it's nothing other than your grief for the big empty spot you've got. You've both got the same empty spot.

Erika: I wanted to give our other two children as normal a life as possible. That was *very* important to me. And how could you do that with their brother dead? And I didn't want our son who died to be ashamed of us. We had to do that for his memory too. I didn't want him to be the cause of our marriage breaking up. I think of his friends. I think we have to set an example for them that you can go on with your life whether you want to or not. And you have to make it meaningful. We have been given a gift of more life, more years on earth.

Emphasizing the Good

Some couples make an effort to remain positive, with each finding ways to praise the other and emphasizing the good things that the partner has done in relationship to the child's dying and death. You need to be real about things. But emphasizing the good helps to create an environment in which you are each giving the other support and affirmation. As you both heal from your grief, you will find that the two of you have developed a shared strength and shared understanding vital for healing your relationship. With that can come a bittersweet sense that what you have gone through together has given you a stronger, deeper, more durable marriage.

Appendix

The Couples and
Their Children Who Died

I PROMISED EVERYONE who was interviewed that I would disguise their identity, so the names listed here are not actual names. In some cases I have further disguised the identity of a couple by changing some other pieces of information. These couples came from a number of U.S. states and two Canadian provinces. The information given for each couple (ages, duration married, time since the death) reflects the situation when the couple was interviewed.

Amy and Ted, ages forty-four and forty-five, married nineteen years. Noah died twelve years ago, age five months, of a genetic disorder.

Becky and Bill, ages fifty-five and fifty-nine, married thirty-three years. Steve died fifteen years ago, age fourteen, of acute alcohol poisoning.

Molly and Earl, ages forty-five and forty-seven, now divorced. Heather and Jacqueline died nineteen years ago, ages three and five, of accidental electrocution.

Joy and Stan, ages thirty-nine and forty, married twenty-five years. Jenny died sixteen years ago, age five and a half, in a car accident.

Sue and Gabe, ages fifty-nine and sixty, married thirty-eight years. Tracy died thirty-two years ago, age one, of cancer.

Glenda and Ken, ages fifty-one and fifty-three, married thirty-four years. Mark died five years ago, age twenty-three, in a car accident.

Erika and Chad, ages forty-eight and fifty-six, married twenty-eight years. David died six years ago, age fourteen, in an autoerotic accident.

Tina and Scott, ages thirty-nine and forty, married sixteen years. Gina died ten years ago, age three days, of a birth defect.

Angela and Jack, ages thirty-five and forty, married two years. Blake died two years ago, age two months, from sudden infant death syndrome (SIDS).

Jane and Rob, ages forty-five and forty-six, married twenty-four years. Adam died thirteen years ago, age two and a half, of cancer or cancer treatment.

Joan and Brett, ages thirty-four and thirty-six, married eight years. Alex died five years ago, age seven months, of complications from premature birth.

Gail and Vince, ages forty-one and forty, married seventeen years. Randy died eight years ago, age two months, from SIDS.

Iris and Todd, ages forty and forty-seven, married sixteen years. Jeff died six years ago, age four months, from birth defects.

Sally and Bruce, ages thirty-three and thirty-eight, married about eight years. Mike died four years ago, age ten days, from birth defects.

Rosa and Henry, ages thirty-seven and thirty-nine, married sixteen years. Wendy died ten years ago, age fifteen months, from birth defects.

Hannah and Fred, ages fifty and fifty-three, married twenty-nine years. Tyler died three years ago, age twenty-three, from suicide.

Kathy and Karl, ages forty-three and forty-four, married twenty-one years. Joel and Ruth died fourteen and twelve years ago, both at three and a half months, of a genetic disorder.

Marsha and Denny, ages thirty-five and thirty-three, married five years. Matt died two years ago at ten weeks of birth defects and complications from premature birth. Ellen was stillborn six months ago.

Kelly and Lance, ages thirty-seven and thirty-five, married nine years. Leanne died four years ago, age five and a half weeks, of birth defects and complications from premature birth.

Lisa and Nick, ages forty-two and forty-one, married twenty-two years. Craig died seven years ago, age thirteen, of a cerebral aneurysm.

Steph and George, ages forty-four and forty-five, married twenty-four years. Nils died five years ago, age five and a half, by accidental drowning.

Louise and Wayne, ages forty-nine and fifty, married twenty-four years. Will died seven years ago, age fourteen, when he was hit by a car.

Bonnie and John, ages fifty-seven and fifty-nine, married about thirty-five years. Jill died one year ago, age thirty-three, of cancer.

Alice and Jay, ages fifty-three and sixty-five, married about thirty-five years. Penny died one year ago, age twenty-nine, in a farm accident.

Candy and Woody, ages fifty-eight and fifty-seven, married thirty-five years. Roland died eight months ago, age twenty-seven, in a farm accident.

Erin and Gene, both age sixty-eight, married about thirty-nine years. Don died thirty-five years ago, age five, in a farm accident.

Paula and Pete, ages thirty-eight and forty, married about eighteen years. Jerry died six years ago, age three, in a farm accident.

Elaine and Red, ages forty-five and fifty, married twenty-seven years. Kyle died eight years ago, age thirteen, in a farm accident.

Barb and Al, ages forty-five and fifty-one, married twenty-five years. Tom died five years ago, age seventeen, in a farm accident.

Index